New Terror, New Wars

Books in the Series

New Terror, New Wars

Paul Gilbert

Edinburgh University Press

© Paul Gilbert, 2003

Edinburgh University Press Ltd
22 George Square, Edinburgh

Typset in Sabon
by TechBooks, and
printed and bound in Great Britain
by Bell & Bain Ltd, Glasgow

A CIP record for this book is available
from the British Library

ISBN 0 7486 1614 4 (paperback)

Contents

Series Preface

The date, the mood of the times, the changed view of what should engage the attention of social philosophers and students of ethics, all combine to suggest that this is the right moment for a book series which aims to make a reasoned contribution to debate about ethical decision-making in many areas of practical policy where the moral map seems unclear and opinion is frequently divided.

To some extent, this is always to be expected, but the start of the third millennium was greeted in the Western world with particular hope and optimism. It was a world eager to put behind it the twentieth century, the first half of which had seen two world wars, the second a period in which the two ideologies of communism and free democracy had remained precariously poised on the brink of mutually assured destruction. The apparent removal of that threat produced a millennial mood of new hope for the future that was reflected in public celebration and a widespread welcome for change; the new, the novel, the innovatory, the modern and the modernising, were key words reflecting these aspirations. And indeed the world *did* change, although it took another year or two to reveal that this was not to be in the benevolent way people had hoped. The events in New York of September 11, 2001 and subsequent developments elsewhere in the world produced a seismic shift in the way the world would be viewed, reversing the complacency that had followed the ending of the Cold War. A new religious divide was opening up between a secularised West with its origins in Judaeo-Christian values and an observant Islam; at the same time, religious divisions attached compulsory labels even to the religiously uncommitted.

One consequence of all this is that it has become clear how far Western values, public and private, shifted in the second half of the twentieth century. Even the first half of that century would not have produced such contrasts in values, expectations and behaviour amongst the main cultural divisions of the world. Dress, customs, marriage traditions, women's role, entertainment – in all these areas, a certain commonality would have prevailed, capable of oiling the wheels of cultural contact and exchange. Currently, though, a widening gulf is to be found in views about what is decent or permissible in the private sphere; and this difference in viewpoint expresses itself publicly in the media, in sexual behaviour, in family policy. At the same time, on the broader stage of states, nations and communities, other differences emerge. Old assumptions about the nature, conditions and justifications of war no longer fit the contemporary world, while concepts of ethnic and national identity have become confused. Individuals and groups in a globalised world have voluntarily uprooted themselves, ignoring traditional territorial boundaries and jurisdictions, and this has forced the desirable destinations of the wealthier West to confront contentious questions concerning refugees, immigration and control of borders.

In another sphere again, the world of scientific research and the pursuit of knowledge, Western science – now a world science – has produced advances on many fronts. One of these is in the technology of war and weaponry; another, discoveries in biomedical areas, especially genetics. The first of these generates new fears and a sense of individual helplessness in the face of threats; the second, new ethical questions concerning the margins of life – questions about how to deal with the extending human life-span, and how to regulate the possibilities that have arisen for controlling new human life at the embryonic stage. Science has also dramatically changed communication and is certain to go on doing so. Computers will be less mechanistic and more biological. They will also be cheaper and more ubiquitous – people in third world countries as well as in the richer developed world will have access to them.

Again, while wars rage between peoples, there are those who predict that a new war-front that will open up will be that of humans versus other forms of life, perhaps even at the bacterial level. The brief period of human dominance of the planet may be coming to an end, aided and precipitated by our careless treatment of the natural environment. On the one hand, then, some would paint a Malthusian picture of the new era, ending in planetary destruction, possibly precipitated by a self-destructive Armageddon. On the other hand, however, there remains the inestimable gift of human reason which, if supported by longstanding values that still command widespread respect, may yet lead us out of the current darkness into a second Enlightenment. The questions remain, however, uneasily unanswerable. Will we use scientific and medical advance for good? Will we be able to take a thoughtful and restrained approach to the world environment? Will we choose to embrace the best rather than the worst aspects of the world's religious heritages? Will we be able to retain and indeed reassert the ethical values, public and private, with which these are linked: the private values of love, trust, faithfulness, duty, modesty, unselfishness, respect for one another; the public values of non-licentious freedom, regard for the rights of the human individual, and the pursuit of the common good?

A thin strand of optimism suggests that open thought and honest reflection may at least contribute towards finding the right answers to these questions. It is this thin strand of optimism that provides a background and a justification for this series of books which address the ethical dimensions of some key controversies of our time. The authors of books in the series, while varied in their views and positions, seek to set out and analyse the most pressing of today's issues, to offer in some cases their own solutions, but also to provide the arguments that will allow their readers to agree or disagree, for that is the privilege and prerogative of reason.

Brenda Almond

Preface

'Writing this book over the last couple of years has been a dispiriting experience.' So I wrote in the Preface to an earlier book, *Terrorism, Security and Nationality* (London: Routledge, 1994). The writing of this one has been scarcely more heartening. Having started by exploring the evidently nationalist violence of the end of the twentieth century and the reactions to it of states and alliances, I struggled to make sense of the breakdown of ethical norms on all sides. Then, halfway through the writing, came September 11 and its aftermath in Afghanistan, which forced me to broaden the scope of the enquiry and to become, perhaps, more politically engaged than I had originally envisaged. The present volume is the result, raising, as it does, many more questions than it answers and eliciting, I dare say, more disagreement than assent.

Chapter 1 contains material presented to a conference on 'War and Virtual War' at Mansfield College, Oxford in 2002, while part of Chapter 3 was given at the Royal Irish Academy, Dublin, 'Philosophy and Psychoanalysis' conference in the same year. Chapter 6 incorporates part of my contribution to the Society of Applied Philosophy conference at Manchester, 2001, which was subsequently published in A. Moseley & R. Norman (eds) *Human Rights and Military Intervention* (Aldershot: Ashgate, 2002). I thank the editors and publishers (www.ashgate.com) for permission to reuse it. The same chapter also draws upon a paper given to a 'Truth, Amnesty and Reconciliation' conference at Hull in 2000. I should like to thank the organisers of these events for the opportunity to think about the issues involved and the participants for their critical reactions.

Foremost among the others to whom I am indebted for illuminating discussion is Loretta Napoleoni, who has been a constant source of encouragement since she translated my earlier terror-ism book into Italian six years ago. I should also like to thank the series editor Brenda Almond, Edinburgh University Press's editor Jackie Jones, my copy-editor Nicola Wood and Hull Humanities secretary Chris Coulson, without whom the book would not have reached the stage of publication. I am grateful, too, to the University of Hull and to the Arts and Humanities Research Board for research leaves which enabled me to write it. My greatest hope is that it will rapidly become irrelevant; my fear is that it will not.

Unless the context indicates otherwise, nouns and pronouns grammatically masculine or feminine are used without specific implications as to the gender of persons to whom they apply.

Paul Gilbert

Old and New Wars

Old wars

Contrast two wars. One, the Falklands conflict of 1982; the other, the so-called 'War on Terror' – the name given to the US-led reaction to the events of September 11, 2001 which we can, for convenience, view as themselves the first strikes in the same war. First, the Falklands conflict is, I want to say, a typical 'old war';[1] and I shall try to outline what I mean by this by citing some of its features. I shall group these into those that characterise what I call the 'conditions' of the war, on the one hand, and what I call its 'conduct' on the other. If we follow Clausewitz's famous dictum that war is the continuation of policy by other means then the conditions represent, broadly speaking, the way that the war is seen as pursuing policy.[2] The conduct of war is the way the war is fought, and this will, evidently, depend to a great extent upon its conditions. What then were the conditions of the Falklands conflict?

The first point to make is that it was a conflict between established states, thus conforming to Rousseau's account of war as: 'something that occurs not between man and man, but between States. The individuals who become involved in it are enemies only by accident.'[3] The Falklands conflict was a war between states because it was a war over territory, to which each claimed a right of sovereignty. Thus on the one side it was viewed as a war against an occupying power, on the other, defence against aggression. Each state sought to occupy or reoccupy the Falklands in order to establish its rule. This was the avowed political purpose of the war so that only those means judged necessary for this purpose were adopted, and, with the purpose accomplished by one side, there was, for that time at any rate, no further reason for military conflict and conditions of peace returned. War, not having been, for the losing side, an effective means of securing the objects of policy, was, at least for the time being, set aside.

The characteristics of the conduct of the war derive from these features. Its military purpose on both sides was unequivocally a victory in armed conflict. The objectives of the forces deployed were therefore military objectives. The actions taken to secure them were calculated as what might be needed in terms of losses both to one's own side and to the other. Those not involved in the conflict – civilians, surrendered combatants and so on – were, for the most part, not the target of hostile action and were given protection from its effects. Two objections that may be made to this account serve only to emphasise its essential point. Surely, it may be objected, the sinking of the *General Belgrano* by a British submarine, with great loss of life, was not necessary to winning the war, since it had remained outside the so-called 'exclusion zone'. And were there not, it is claimed, atrocities against Argentinian POWs, contrary to the customs of war? Suppose, as I can allow, that both contentions are true. The way that they were made, at the time and after, as protests against the conduct of the war from the British side, presupposes, rather than contradicts, the fact that the war was being conducted essentially along the lines I have described. It is as possible deviations that these events were protested against, not as characterising the whole conduct of the war. For it is as acts of unnecessary savagery that they were condemned, not as serving some further purpose.

A similar riposte can be made to a possible earlier objection that the Falklands War was itself unnecessary, that policy, on either side, did not dictate it and its costs, on each side, were too great. All of this may well be true, but again it presupposes rather than contradicts my account of the conditions of the war. For what is not called into question is that the proper purpose of such a war is to hold territory in which to govern, which was the avowed purpose of the war. To the extent to which the war was unnecessary, too risky or too costly to secure this purpose, other motives may be suspected – that the victor's 'greatness will increase as a result', perhaps, to quote Machiavelli.[4] But again this is the sort of deviation which presupposes that the conditions of war as I have described them are the norm for conflicts like that over the Falklands, and thus that the fulfilment of these conditions must be defended in relation to this norm. The norms that I have sketched are, as I shall spell out later in more detail, the norms for what I am calling here 'old wars'.

New wars

Contrast with this the so-called War on Terror and the terroristic counterpart which makes it a two-sided war, starting with its conditions.[5] First, the War on Terror is not a straightforward war between states, but between a state, or combination of states, on one side and non-state actors on the other. This is, we may say, its basic structure, though the reality is more complex, with the supposed state sponsors of terror also being targeted, and sometimes targeted through the use of proxy non-state fighters. What, then, is the war about? This is much more difficult to determine than in the Falklands conflict. That was a war in which states were in disagreement and in which each sought to discharge its responsibility to govern in its own territory. In this the purposes, on both sides, are altogether higher. On the one hand, a variety of Islamic groups see themselves as reclaiming Muslim lands from the infidel or from his influence. On the other, the US, its allies, and others who have taken its war to be their own, proclaim a battle for various values which we can, without prejudice, call Western – freedom, democracy, and 'civilisation' itself, with its presumed respect for the value of human life and equal dignity.

What I want to emphasise about such aims is that they are, on neither side, those that are essentially connected with the discharge of a state's responsibilities. For a state exists for the government of its citizens and to defend the borders of a territory within which they can be governed. It does not exist to promote a particular set of values or way of life. It may well do that, internally or internationally, but in so doing it is going beyond those functions which make it a state. It is, then, an accident that one of the parties in the war on terrorism is a state, or a combination of states, so far as the political purposes of the war are concerned. Rather, just as the Islamic groups claim authority for their struggle from Koranic law and Muslim tradition, so the anti-terrorist states claim theirs on the basis of being institutions which protect the values they promote. In each case the authority that is claimed is authority to act on behalf of a group identified in terms of their values in order to rectify a wrong perpetrated against them by those who lack these values.

This has implications for the way that war is thought to achieve its purpose. Unlike a war waged to secure the borders of a territory for peaceful government, a war fought to deliver justice has no clear limits and there is no clear relationship between its political goals and its efficacy as a means of achieving them. Just as no police force is ever stood down, since crime is never ended, so on neither side in the War on Terror is there any clear indication of what would terminate the war, since the perceived injustices on both sides are likely to continue so long as there is conflict over where justice lies. Correspondingly, it is unclear how war, specifically, is required for, and suitable to, delivering justice, and thus how its effectiveness or otherwise is to be assessed for the purposes of determining whether it needs or ought to be continued with as an instrument of policy. On neither side, in consequence, is it easy to see the use of force otherwise than as primarily a reaction to perceived injustices and waged to express such perceptions.

The conduct of the War on Terror is partly determined by these conditions, very different as they are from those of the Falklands conflict. In the former war it is, as I have indicated, hard to see what victory would amount to, nor is it clear that purely military victory is what those fighting the war are aiming to achieve. Rather, on either side it is as much the ordinary people of each side as their combatants whom the use of force is designed to affect. On the Islamist side the aim is retribution for crimes against Islam perpetrated by the Americans and their allies; on the American side it is, retribution for crimes perpetrated by radical Muslims against Americans and others expressing a Western lifestyle. It follows that all those who are guilty of these supposed crimes must feel themselves to be attacked, not just those engaged in military operations. This can be accomplished either by directly targeting civilians, as in Islamist terrorism, or by attacks on combatants which cause their civilian supporters loss of life, injury and destruction of property. The result in either case is the application of pressure to make them repent of and desist from involvement or complicity in the alleged injustices.

The other factor determining the conduct of the War on Terror is the great disparity in conventional military strength arising from the fact that it is a conflict between the forces of a state or states on the one hand and those of principally non-state actors on the other, with, at most, the support of weak states or the covert and qualified support of somewhat stronger ones. This results in the asymmetry of the war: the Islamist side adopting terrorist and guerrilla tactics – hence the name conferred on the conflict by the other side, whose own tactics involve the use both of sophisticated surveillance techniques and of overwhelming force with very little risk to its own personnel, so-called 'virtual war'.[6] On each side attacks on clearly military objectives may not, therefore, be the primary focus of operations: on the Islamist, because they lack the military capacity, except for strikes on a US warship and US servicemen's quarters in Arabia; on the American, because when the Islamists are in their characteristic terrorist mode, they seldom present any distinct military targets, and must, in consequence, either be pursued through policing methods, rather than engaged in combat, or be denied the use of large areas through subjecting them to extensive bombing, as in Afghanistan.

It will no doubt be objected to this account of the War on Terror that it exaggerates the difference from the Falklands conflict by failing to acknowledge that each is, on one or both sides, a war of self-defence. This is an objection which I shall take up later. But what I want to emphasise is the distinction I am drawing between the military defence of a territory for the peaceable governance of the citizens within it and the defence of a group of people in virtue of their collective identity. The Falklands War instantiates the former, reflecting the international law perspective that the use of military force is permissible for self-defence of this sort but, broadly speaking, not otherwise;[7] so that the question which arose was whether it was Argentina or Britain which had the right so to use force. The War on Terror, I am claiming, instantiates the latter.

That is to say, it is, on the one side, *qua* Muslims that Islamist groups are claiming to defend the people they supposedly represent: they are defending them not just as individuals subjected to physical violence and oppression at the hands of the US and its agents, but as Muslims whose religion and way of life are under threat, and who are subjected to harm precisely on account of their religion.[8] The US claims are the counterpart of these, despite the fact that, unlike the Islamists, the US government asserts its right of self-defence under international law and hence must present the conflict in a way that arguably conforms to these requirements. For it is not just as individuals exposed to risk of harm that it mounts its military campaign in their defence: it is not just as US citizens for whom it is responsible, but as people with a way of life that expresses certain values, so that these values themselves are taken to be under threat and their beneficiaries exposed to danger precisely in pursuance of this threat.[9]

It is for this reason that American action abroad, in common with that in many new wars, has the character of military intervention, that is to say of action directed not against a state as such, on account of its claims or alliances and, in virtue of these, entitled to rely on the support of its citizens, but either against a regime which flouts certain values or in disregard of one that fails to uphold them. Again this parallels the action of Muslim terrorists, for, as I indicated earlier, it is not in virtue of America's actions *as* a state that it is attacked, but as the vanguard for a system of values taken to be antithetical to Islam.

Contrasting conditions

I should now like to draw together more systematically some of the features of these wars in order to point up the contrast between old and new, bearing in mind, of course, that, though these two wars are in many respects typical, others will differ from them in various ways. We have here, I suggest, only family resemblances between members of the two classes, which are, for all that, useful analytical tools.

Old wars are typically wars between states, seeking to promote the interests that states have *qua* states – secure borders and other conditions for a peaceful, prosperous and orderly life. When one side or more is not a state, as in civil wars, this is because some portion of the citizenry does not feel that it enjoys such conditions and seeks to establish these, either by effecting a change in the existing political order within the states' current borders or by changing these borders, as in secessionist struggles pursued solely because of the circumstances in which one side finds itself. New wars, by contrast, may be regarded as wars between or on behalf of peoples, in the sense that the sides in the war are identified in terms of identities that are given, not just through membership of states or potential states, but through membership of groups whose representatives advance political claims – including claims to separate statehood – in virtue of the kinds of people of which these groups consist.

There are a multitude of cases here. The simplest is one where two groups identify themselves as separate and where their conflicts are an expression of discord between them, as, at least at some times, between Muslims and Hindus in the Indian subcontinent, for example. Partition was intended to address a conflict conceptualised in these terms, though it left a continuing legacy of bitterness with respect to Kashmir and otherwise. Many secessionist struggles have this character, but not all, even when they are identity conflicts. For in some cases, a state will oppose secession precisely because it cannot grant that the secessionists are a separate people, so that now the conflict concerns not what should be accorded to peoples acknowledged to be separate, but what acknowledgement of separate identities should be made. And such acknowledgement, or its refusal, is sought from the people themselves as well as from their states and other political organisations; for self-identification is needed if people are to be mobilised behind a military campaign, though the existence of such a campaign can itself influence self-identification.

The War on Terror is of this sort. Whereas the Islamists regard it as a war between peoples identified as Muslims on the one hand and non-Muslims generally on the other, the Americans and their allies deny they are fighting against Muslims. They view Muslims as identified in terms not of their religion but of their nationality as given by language, territorial affiliation or whatever, just as Westerners are so viewed. But such identities are quite compatible with overarching attachments to values of freedom, democracy and so on, which Islamist hard-liners are taken to reject. There is thus an ideological struggle between the Islamists and US allies to win over ordinary Muslims to the one kind of identity or the other. On the Islamist side the war is viewed as a conflict *between* peoples; on the American, as fought by them *on behalf of* those peoples who are taken to espouse the prescribed values, but whose identities as such are threatened by those that reject them. In either case, I suggest, the war concerns the manner in which collective identities should be politically recognised, and this is a feature I take to be necessary to anything that is to count as a new war.

That new wars concern the manner in which collective identities should be politically recognised reflects, I want to say, discord rather than disagreement – in the simplest cases, as just mentioned, discord between peoples viewing themselves as separate; in the more complex ones, discord prior and contributory to any possible demarcation of separateness. Discord is categorically different from disagreement, since it characterises the state of a relationship rather than an event within it, even though, of course, discord can easily generate disagreements and vice versa. Discord between peoples can exist, however, without being the obvious result of any disagreement and can issue in violence or even war. Between states the case is otherwise. Their old wars are typically and explicitly the upshot of disagreements not peaceably resolved, of which disagreements about territory or spheres of influence are, perhaps, the commonest.

Discord is characteristically either a consequence of the possession of different values or gives rise to a highlighting of real or imagined differences in values, so that the actions of one group are seen as affronts to the values of the other, as failures to show the respect that is due and, hence, as injustices. There is, therefore, a direct connection between the fact that new wars are expressions of discord, as I have put it, and that they take the form of campaigns for justice, rather than merely the securing of peaceful and orderly lives for bodies of citizens. While old wars are, of course, fought for ends represented as just, these ends are limited, as I have tried to show, to those to which citizen bodies are generally taken to be entitled, so that the disagreements which occasion old wars are typically disagreements over the precise character of these entitlements and whether they have been fulfilled, all taking place within a framework of agreement as to their general nature. In new wars the case is quite different. For without any such framework of agreement, indeed, precisely in a situation of discord in respect of values, a campaign for justice is not merely a manifestation of self-help in the absence of an authority to arbitrate on competing claims, it is itself an expression of the possession of superior authority to administer justice against those who transgress its demands.

Contrasting conduct

If the conditions of new wars, then, are that they are fought against or on behalf of peoples, over the manner in which their collective identities should be politically recognised, as expressions of discord and as campaigns for justice, then we may expect the characteristic features of their conduct to reflect this, as in the particular example we started with. Thus, whereas old wars are directed against states or other citizen bodies through attacks on their armed forces, new ones are aimed at identity groups or those who seek to constitute such groups. They are, therefore, fought in ways that either directly target members of these groups, *qua* members rather than *qua* combatants, or neglect their welfare, while often evincing disproportionate concern for that of members of one's own group. Attacks of this kind are often direct and violent means towards or against the political recognition that is sought. The most obvious case is that of 'ethnic cleansing' in which ordinary people are attacked to force them from an area, either to reserve it to another identity group or to make it unavailable to one that espouses a separate or proscribed identity with political claims.

Attacks on or affecting ordinary people are easily accomplished in the atmosphere of discord surrounding new wars, which has two further related consequences for their conduct. Just as attacks upon civilians, or those that disproportionately affect them, are contrary to the rules of war, so too is the mistreatment of enemy combatants, whether through killings on a scale that has no military purpose or through the killing, torture or cruel incarceration of prisoners. Yet this is exactly what we witness in new wars, where discord obliterates respect for an enemy. One reason for the breaking of rules is that on one side, at least, troops are commonly irregulars, untrained, undisciplined and often without a clear chain of command terminating in political control. Recruitment to such irregular units is facilitated by discord and by mobilisation behind the cause of an identity group. By their nature such units are unlikely to be equipped for conventional warfare, and are forced to resort to guerrilla or terrorist tactics with all their dangers. Asymmetric struggles thus characterise new wars. But it should not be thought that the regular forces of states thereby escape the evils I have mentioned. Discord affects them too, and the massive counterforce they can employ is as much an expression of it as are terrorist attacks.

Lastly, however, the presentation of the causes of identity groups as the delivery of justice, in the particular way I have sought to specify, can be used to excuse many of the excesses of new wars and disguise discord and hatred behind a veil of righteous indignation. Whereas in old wars non-combatants and combatants *hors de combat* are not to be targeted because they do not, by their intentional actions, obstruct military operations to secure territory, in new wars they may be just as implicated in the supposed injustice the war is intended to rectify as are their soldiers in action. They may, for example, in an obvious case, be occupying territory claimed by another identity group. In a less obvious one, they may be willing beneficiaries of policies that threaten the way of life of an identity group, as Islamists evidently take the American people to be. In such cases, a new war, construed as a campaign for justice, may evidently take such people as targets or, at least, as not deserving of the sorts of protection offered in old wars.

Campaigns for justice also involve different tactics from those of old wars, in which it is accepted, at least in inter-state conflicts, that the armed forces of each side have a right to resist attack, however justified, since they are simply carrying out their leaders' orders as soldiers. It is otherwise in new wars, where resisting attack is obstructing justice, in the same way that resisting the forces of law and order compounds the felony which those forces are seeking to rectify. Thus, while in old wars retaliation must have a military purpose to be justified, in new wars it serves simply to rectify yet a further perceived injustice. Since each side will take the same view of its own superior authority to deliver justice, there ensues the apparently endless tit-for-tat attacks without any clear purpose which we witness in new wars. And, of course, these are as often aimed at other members of the group as at those who have launched the original attack. For it is the identity group as a whole, or at least its active supporters, who are taken to be 'engaged in an objectively unjust proceeding',[10] not just particular attackers, as would be the case with ordinary felons.

Roles and identities

New wars, I have claimed, are, essentially, manifestations of the politics of identity. Their participants are groups which possess, or for which are claimed, distinctive collective identities; and they concern, in one way or another, the manner in which such identities should be recognised. What the politics of identity presupposes is that one enters political life as a person with a particular collective identity. This, it has been held, is a view deriving from German Romantic nationalism – 'I am essentially a German, and I am a man through my being a German' – though arguably it has an older, and ultimately religious, pedigree.[11] That one enters politics as the possessor of a particular identity supposedly makes it appropriate that a political organisation, like a state, or, perhaps, a combination of states, should associate one with others who share that identity. It is this identity, furthermore, that equips one with the values one must employ in political action, and maybe outside of it as well. And what goes for politics generally goes for that continuation of politics which is war. New wars are fought by agents *qua* possessors of identities, real or imagined,[12] acting on behalf of their identity groups and in accordance with their values.

What I want to contrast with the politics of identity is an earlier – at least in recent times – 'politics of role', as I shall call it.[13] The politics of role presupposes that I enter politics without any essential collective identity but as someone set to perform a specific role, most usually, in the modern political world, the role of a citizen. One does not, that is to say, enter politics with prior attributes which the character of one's political relationships should reflect, but rather one's relationships are shaped by the way one performs one's role. How one ought to act in the political arena is not determined by values anterior to its activities, but by the duties required by the role, which, therefore, carry no implications for how one ought to act outside of it. It is, in a useful slogan, *what* one is which determines how one should act in the politics of role; *who* one is, in the politics of identity.

Typical old wars are, to paint the picture in broad brushstrokes, contests between states in which the various actors behave in ways regulated by the requirements of their roles. The leaders of states act to secure their states' vital interests while respecting the norms of international relations which make possible a range of exchanges between states, including, when peaceful dialogue breaks down, warlike ones. Leaders are, in so acting, representing people *qua* citizens – persons performing a role for which the security of the state is a precondition. Members of the state's armed forces, usually citizens themselves, have their roles too. Their task is to fight opposing forces through methods calculated to achieve military victory, which are limited to those proportionate to such goals and discriminating in their targets, so that civilians and surrendered troops are not made the object of attack. The conduct of war is, then, in the hands of soldiers, sailors and airmen and its rules are those that constrain the holders of these roles. The conditions of war in old wars, likewise, are also governed by rules – rules about when it is permissible to resort to war and not be engaging in impermissible aggression. These international norms are what constrain the behaviour of those who occupy the role of statesmen or other relevant political leaders. It is rules in respect of both the conditions and conduct of war that get set aside when the politics of role gives way to the politics of identity.

To illustrate this process consider what happened in Azerbaijan as the Soviet Union fell apart in the late 1980s. In the earlier part of the decade the citizens of Azerbaijan were supporting their compatriot, Gary Kasparov, in his chess contests with the Russian, Anatoly Karpov, 'regardless of the fact that Kasparov was half Armenian and half Jewish, without a drop of Azerbaijani blood'.[14] By the end of the decade, however, Armenians and Azerbaijanis were locked in a civil war in which ethnic cleansing claimed thousands of lives and displaced hundreds of thousands as each side claimed Nagorno-Karabakh as part of its own historic homeland. It was to be the pattern of things to come as the Cold War balance of power broke down and nationalist movements across the world backed their claims with armed force. Identity politics had come to dominate conflict.

In the early 1980s, however, the people of Azerbaijan were acting as citizens in supporting the ethically non-Azeri Kasparov. One of the expectations from those who perform the role of citizen is support for fellow citizens, even in sporting contests. But when ethnic Armenians and Azeris began to clash within the state they shared as citizens they were no longer performing these roles. It is not that civil war itself makes this impossible. When one body of citizens within a state is being oppressed by another it can rise up in revolt, either to overthrow a government that permits this or to secede, and in either case those engaged in the conflict can be acting as citizens, their leaders as representative of citizens, and their forces as the armies of citizen bodies striving for military victory. But when the civil war concerns the manner in which collective identities shall be politically recognised, as in the conflict over Nagorno-Karabakh, the participants are not acting as citizens with the interests proper to citizens in mind, but simply as members of identity groups. And the way that this conflict was fought out reflects that, with all the discord and consequent excess that new wars entail.

Identity politics and role politics are, I am suggesting, distinct modes of political activity, in the sense that participants conceive of themselves and of what is expected of them differently in the two modes. They are answerable to different ethical demands and regulate their behaviour differently accordingly, whether or not they have any clear, conscious conception of their relevant identity or role. Yet in any actual political situation there may also be practical unclarity as to which mode of politics is in play, with participants sometimes adopting the one, sometimes the other. The Arab/Israeli conflict is a prime example of this, with what is fundamentally an old war about the rights of an oppressed group, as against an established state's demand for security, degenerating into an identity conflict between Jews and Muslims. It would, therefore, be wrong to think of old and new wars as clear historical categories, with a transition from the former to the latter representing a sea change from role to identity politics.[15] Rather it represents, I am suggesting, a shift of emphasis in recent years from one prevailing mode to another, and with it a loss of previously accepted standards of behaviour, particularly in war, however much these standards were in fact flouted.[16] Each mode is, in the right historical circumstances, a possibility at any one time, so that the transition from the one mode to another is not a purely recent phenomenon.

The politics of role is, indeed, an essentially classical conception, deriving from Greek models of citizenship and coming to fruition in Roman notions of this status as available quite independently of group identity. This conception is drawn upon in later times, most especially after the establishment of the Westphalian system of sovereign states, which put an end to the religious wars of the seventeenth century by establishing a principle of military non-intervention and other norms of international relations, many of which are now codified in the United Nations Charter.[17]

The key point about these norms is that they are transcultural. They have to be if they are to regulate relations between states whose members will often come from widely diverse cultural backgrounds. Thus the role of a statesman, or comparable political leader, is constrained by international norms which allow holders to communicate and negotiate with each other on the basis of common understandings of what they are doing and what the permissible moves are. The same holds good for the role of soldier. A soldier's role is circumscribed by norms which permit military engagements to take place against a shared background of what constitutes such an engagement and how it is to be undertaken. To deviate substantially from such norms is no longer to occupy the roles, but to adopt a quite different kind of persona, perhaps that of the charismatic leader or warrior of identity politics. But whereas the norms of international roles are the result of transcultural interactions, in which certain standards have come to be fixed, what is expected of a charismatic leader or a warrior by their particular identity groups depends solely on the values which that group possesses, providing no scope for international criticism or regulation without the danger of an affront to these values.

Just war and defence

It will come as no surprise to learn that the international norms governing the roles played out in old wars are those of what is thought of as the just war.[18] Just war theory distinguishes two sets of requirements for a war to be accounted 'just'. The first are the requirements for *jus ad bellum* – for having a right to go to war; the second, for *jus in bello* – for right conduct in war. Now, the *jus ad bellum* requirements are, I claim, precisely the constraints that are placed upon statesmen and comparable political leaders when they decide whether to embark upon a war; the *jus in bello* ones, those placed upon soldiers and other troops involved in one. In each case, and perhaps most clearly in the latter, what it is to perform the role is determined in part by a preparedness to adhere to these requirements. Let us, then, rehearse them in relation to what I have termed, respectively, the conditions and conduct of war. The just war theory which results will, for reasons that will become obvious, be a 'defensive' just war theory, and that is how I shall term it.

Consider first, then, the requirement that a war is just only if it is decided upon by *proper authority*. This may be taken to spell out the relationship which a leader who decides upon war must have to those on whose behalf it is fought. In general, it will be a constitutional relationship between statesman and state, so that the party to the war is the state itself, rather than the forces of the state being unofficially employed on behalf of some faction. Yet, as I indicated earlier, in exceptional circumstances, a leader may represent a body of citizens who do not constitute a state, as when they find themselves oppressed by one and rise up against it. This brings us to the second requirement, that of *just cause*. This, in defensive just war theory, is provided only by the war being fought in self-defence, though what amounts to self-defence can, of course, be controversial, depending upon who has the better claim to defend a given territory. But whoever it is, the purpose must, as we have seen, be to secure the territory for the purpose of governing its citizens in a lawful manner and in their own interests.

The other requirements of *jus ad bellum* follow from this and point up the role of a statesman in relation to the citizens he represents. Thus forming a *right intention* involves aiming to restore a situation of peace in which all citizens, whoever they are, can live ordered lives. The various requirements that war should be a *proportionate response* to threat, engaged in as a *last resort* and with a fair *hope of success*, all reflect the responsibility of the statesman to his own citizens and to the statesmen of other countries with analogous responsibilities. For war is always an evil, to be avoided wherever possible, not to be resorted to beyond what is strictly necessary and only where effective in restoring peace and security to citizens. To decide on war otherwise than with these requirements in mind is to endanger one's own citizens for reasons that go beyond those that derive from what one owes them. It is also to put one's fellow statesmen in a position where they will find it harder to discharge their responsibilities to their own citizens and hence it is to act in a way that defies rules that exist in order to facilitate the performance of the role of statesman.

Similar considerations apply to the requirements that must be satisfied for *jus in bello* which defensive just war theory imposes upon soldiers. Since, if its cause is just, a war is fought to defend a territory against loss to an enemy, it follows that the role of soldiers is to do what is needed to repel enemy forces and prevent incursions. The requirements of *proportionality* and *discrimination* are consequences of this.[19] Military action is proportionate insofar as it employs only such force as is needed to secure military objectives. Anything more cannot be directed at military victory but at some other end which it is no part of a soldier's job to achieve. Discrimination involves targeting only military objectives, and that implies not attacking civilians, or enemy soldiers *hors de combat*. Again, targeting them, or, indeed, treating them badly in any way, cannot serve ends which it is part of a soldier's role to accomplish. And those who are exempt from attack include, it must be added, the political leaders of the enemy.

Defensive just war theory is, broadly speaking, that which is enshrined in international law, whether customary or codified. Here the fact that international law follows the *practice* of states – a feature often regarded as quite extraordinary – actually brings out the way in which it is shaped by actual exchanges between entities whose leaders have a common interest in peace as well as particular interests in maintaining their own states' security and power.[20] The result is two bodies of law: that which relates to the permissible use of force, as spelt out in the UN Charter and the resolutions which interpret it; and that which covers the conduct of war, as set forth in the Hague and Geneva Conventions and their various codicils. The former clearly relates to the role of statesmen or other political leaders, the latter to the role of the soldier or member of the other armed forces. It is to these bodies of law which we turn in making ethical assessments of the actions of statesmen and soldiers, and rightly so, for what we are assessing is the propriety of their role performances, and that is, in large measure, determined by their adherence to these laws.

Just war and punishment

Yet what I have termed defensive just war theory is not the only version. There is another with which it is often confused, especially when Christian thinkers, and those influenced by them, debate the justice of a war. There is insufficient space here to do more than sketch out the relationship between them, but we can glimpse it in the contrast between Cicero's and Augustine's conceptions of a just war. Cicero's is defensive: 'There being two sorts of disputing in the world', he observes:

> the one by reason, and the other by open force...when we cannot obtain what is right by the one, we must of necessity have recourse to the other...but it must always be with the design of obtaining a secure peace.[21]

War is rightly waged, then, if all else fails, in defence of a political community's vital interests and must stop at that. St Augustine, by contrast, sees war as the punishment of a wrong, for 'wars are defined as just when their aim is to avenge injury',[22] so that it is an offence against a people's sense of what is right, rather than any objectively specifiable harm, that will lead them to what they conceive as a just war.

This 'punitive' just war theory, as I shall term it, passed into Christian thinking and into that of other religious groups. Thus the medieval crusades provide an example of wars supposedly just on Augustinian criteria, though not on Ciceronian ones, for the perceived injustice being punished and rectified was the injury that Muslims did to Christians by occupying lands sanctified by the presence of Christ.[23] An analogous consideration is in play in contemporary Muslim campaigns to expel the infidel from the lands of Islam.[24] It was precisely this sort of thinking that was held to justify the religious wars that followed the Reformation, whose participants identified themselves in terms of their religious affiliations. These wars were ended only by the Treaty of Westphalia in 1648, which marked a return to a more classical model of politics and put in place the state system which provided the framework, as I have already remarked, for modern role politics.

What, though, are the essential features of punitive just war theory? It contrasts with the defensive version, not in the nominal requirements that are specified for *jus ad bellum* and *jus in bello*, but in the way that these requirements are interpreted. Thus *proper authority* consists in being able to adjudicate on whether serious public wrongs have been perpetrated, so that the emphasis falls on a leader's capacity to articulate and implement his people's values. Having a *just cause* consists in being a victim of wrongful acts, as judged against those values, and having a *right intention* in aiming to deliver justice. By contrast with the defensive theory, none of this has anything essentially to do with a leader's relationship to a body of people. Granted, the traditional theory reserves proper authority to a prince, unless he is a tyrant. But this is for theological reasons having to do with the prince being God's representative on earth in the administration of justice, not the people's.[25]

The other requirements of *jus ad bellum* in punitive theory follow from these. That war be a *proportionate* and *ultimate* sanction, and an *effective* one express the ideas that the punishment should fit the crime, and not be vengeful; that war should be resorted to only when other attempts to bring to justice the perpetrators of wrongs fail; and that war should succeed in rectifying the injustice, for otherwise evil triumphs. Similarly the *in bello* provisions reflect the war's retributive purposes. Proportionality in the conduct of the war is not judged in relation to purely military objectives but in relation to what is deemed necessary for delivering justice. Thus a so-called proportionate response need serve no military purpose in preventing or deterring further attack, so long as it constitutes retaliation not entirely out of scale with the attack to which it responds. Discrimination of response involves not targeting the innocent, that is to say, those who play no part in the original wrong or in obstructing its redress. Evidently, then, civilians are not immune, and, in particular, the leaders and active supporters of the policy that causes the wrong are not; nor are members of the armed forces not, for whatever reason, currently engaged in combat, since they are involved in perpetrating the wrong and preventing its rectification.

Now, it is this punitive version of just war theory, I want to suggest, that has come to the fore in new wars, with the rise of identity politics. Not, of course, that this will be readily acknowledged. For the defensive version is so engrained in international practice that those who can with any plausibility represent their actions as conforming to it will do so, while denying that their opponents have the benefit of any ethical justification for their war at all. The ethical position is, however, a good deal more symmetrical than this. For in new wars, I am claiming, both sides are measuring rights and wrongs by reference to their own values, not by any transcultural standards. Each then takes itself to have proper authority and just cause by the criteria of punitive theory, and each conducts the war largely on the lines that are entailed by its application. The reason why the other side's actions seem so wrong is that, judged by one's own values, indeed they are: it is, for example, the innocent who are targeted, in one's own eyes, in a cause that, far from being just, pursues odious objectives. Without the shared framework provided by role politics, there can be no resolution of such oppositions, nor any standards for the regulation of the wars they foment.

A war on terror?

Let us return, then, in conclusion, to the War on Terror. Terrorism of the sort we witness in new wars is not, it should be apparent from my thesis, some superficial phenomenon, but a particular manifestation of a very deep-seated one. It is identity politics itself which leads the participants in new wars to suppose that terrorist acts, or other excesses, are justifiable, since it is only from the perspective of a politics of role that they are not. Yet identity politics is routinely appealed to in mobilising support for a particular political organisation or combination. The classic cases of this are, as hinted earlier, those species of nationalism which elicit allegiance to a state – actual or potential – on the grounds that it is the state which belongs to a people in virtue of their pre-existing identity, more especially when what is distinctive of that identity is characterised in terms of adherence to a particular set of values. An example already alluded to is the partition of India to create a specifically Muslim state of Pakistan. But identity politics is brought into play as often by established states wishing to strengthen their support as by secessionist movements seeking new states. Indeed, it has become the common currency of contemporary politics when questions of whether there is a popular mandate for the political organisation of a body of citizens arise.

Nor are nationalist causes, narrowly construed, the only case of this. Islamist movements are not conventionally considered to be nationalist, since they seek a style of political organisation for Muslims wider than that of the putative nation states most currently occupy and based, unlike these, on religion rather than ethnicity or territorial attachment. However, even without wishing to destabilise the existing order of states, a political movement may attempt to engender a sense of shared identity in order to mobilise support behind a cause. The medieval crusades were themselves a case of this, seeking to harness a common

Christian identity under papal authority and thereby to sub-ordinate local allegiances. The American-led War on Terror – at one time carelessly referred to by President Bush as itself a crusade – presents some parallels with this. For, as I claimed at the outset, it aims to establish the existence of a 'civilised' identity under threat from another, and, by implication, bar-barous one, which must be prevented from gaining, or retaining, control of political organisations at the level of, or comparable to, states.

The aim is, of course, to corral as many people as possible into the privileged species of identity, not only to gain support for the alliance against terror, but also to ensure a continuing mandate for states constituted from those groups regarded as marked out by identities subordinate to the privileged overarching one. What is more, people are forced into the identity politics mode by the assertion that those who are not for the alliance are against it, excluding the possibility of participation in politics in a way that does not require a commitment to certain specified values. The danger of this approach is evident. It is that, once forced into the identity politics mode and rejecting the privileged identity as an alien imposition, people will support the prohibited identity as they would not previously have done. No doubt this is the calculation of its militant protagonists.

Whether or not this happens, however, the damage has, I sug-gest, already been done. The importation of identity politics into a state's conflict with a group whose grievances can themselves fuel the formation of a collective identity will make it impossible to follow the rules that characterise old wars. A new set of ex-pectations will be generated in which terrorism is an ever-present possibility, since the deeper identification goes, the sharper does discord become, and the greater the outrages that ensue, the more convincing the criminalisation of one's opponent's actions that constitutes them as terrorist. To mobilise a collective identity against terror is then, I claim, essentially counter-productive. For it is precisely to accept a mode of politics in which terror is not an aberration but a norm.

In this introductory chapter I have sketched out freely a set of contrasts which I take to characterise old and new wars. Reality, as I have said, is far more complicated than such glib dichotomies can easily capture. The point of drawing them, however, is to suggest the effects of different ways in which the participants in the making and conducting of wars can see themselves. This helps us, I claim, to view military events as such effects and hence to discern their place in distinctive patterns of social practice. In the case of old wars these practices are familiar to us; and even in new ones those of our own side will, to a greater or lesser extent, also be so, but those of the other side will not, accounting, in part, for our incomprehension and horror at them.

Yet if the distinction as I draw it is to have this sort of utility then it must have some plausible application, at least to some aspects of the wars we currently find troubling as against the ones which, relatively speaking, we do not, and this may be denied. To start with, the scope of self-defence as a cause for war may, as hinted earlier, be alleged to be much more extensive than I have allowed, so that my claim that new wars do not have this character either fails or many wars we would otherwise classify as new are not. This is an objection I take up in the chapter that follows. Next, it may be said, the account I give of identity politics is unduly unsympathetic. Do not at least some kinds of identity groups have a good case for independent government and, if they are then wrongfully denied it, does this not provide them with a just cause for war? The third chapter deals with this issue. Finally, it may be objected that I am too sympathetic to role politics itself, which, some might say, both allows the state too much latitude in internal affairs and restricts other agencies too much in international ones. While I address this approach directly in the last two chapters, I aim along the way to demonstrate some of the merits of retaining, or returning to, a politics of role wherever this is now feasible. Old wars, however horrible, are ethically manageable as new wars are not.

Notes

1. The old war/new war distinction originates, I believe, with Mary Kaldor, *New and Old Wars* (Cambridge: Polity, 1999). Kaldor sees only old wars as exemplifying the Clausewitzian characterisation which follows.
2. Carl von Clausewitz, *On War* [1832] (Harmondsworth: Penguin, 1968), bk. 1, ch. 1, sec. 24, p. 119.
3. Jean Jacques Rousseau, *The Social Contract* (many editions, 1762), bk. 1, ch. 4.
4. Quoted A.J. Coates, *The Ethics of War* (Manchester: Manchester University Press, 1997), p. 162.

5. The account of the War on Terror offered here is, of course, controversial. For some supporting opinions see Phil Scruton (ed.), *Beyond September 11: an Anthology of Dissent* (London: Pluto, 2002).

6. See Michael Ignatieff, *Virtual War* (London: Chatto & Windus, 2000).

7. See Christine Gray, *International Law and the Use of Force* (Oxford: Oxford University Press, 2000), ch. 4.

8. See the 'World Islamic Front Statement' of Osama Bin-Laden (23 February 1998, reproduced in John Kelsay, 'War, Peace and Justice in Islamic Tradition' in Paul Robinson (ed.), *Just War in Comparative Perspective* (Aldershot: Ashgate, forthcoming).

9. See the letter 'What We're Fighting For' (New York: Institute for American Values, February 2002).

10. G.E.M. Anscombe, *Collected Philosophical Papers* (Oxford: Blackwell, 1981), p. 53.

11. Louis Dumont, *Essays in Individualism* (Chicago: University of Chicago Press, 1986), pp. 130–1.

12. Benedict Anderson claims that *all* national identities are, in a sense, imagined: *Imagined Communities* (London: Verso, 1991). That is not the sense in which I use the notion here.

13. '*Role* is not a well-defined and well-developed moral idea, and we will learn to make do with some sloppiness around the edges' Arthur Isak Applbaum, *Ethics for Adversaries: the Morality of Roles in Public and Professional Life* (Princeton: Princeton University Press, 1999), p. 46. Applbaum is one of few recent philosophers to explore the ethics of role since Dorothy Emmett, *Rules, Roles and Relations* (London: Macmillan, 1966). The notion is widely used in sociology, particularly in the symbolic interactionism deriving from G.H. Mead and influential in the work of Erving Goffman.

14. See Arkadii Popov, 'Ethnic Wars in the Transcaucasus', in M. Kaldor & B. Vashee (eds), *New Wars* (London: Pinter, 1997), p. 185.

15. *Pace* Mary Kaldor, *New and Old Wars* who employs the distinction, unlike me, in a literal, chronological sense.

16. E.g. in World War II, which, although an inter-state war, had a strong strain of identity politics that accounted for many of its excesses.

17. Antonio Cassese, however, discerns a distinction between the Westphalian and UN Charter models of international relations. *Self-Determination of Peoples: A Legal Reappraisal* (Cambridge: Cambridge University Press, 1995), p. 325.

18. See my *Terrorism, Security and Nationality* (London: Routledge, 1994), ch. 2.

19. Notice the distinction between proportionality as a requirement of *jus ad bellum* and as a constraint on *jus in bello*.

20. See Geoffrey Best, *War and Law since 1945* (Oxford: Clarendon Press, 1994), pp. 5–10.

21. Cicero, *The Offices* (London: Dent, 1909), I xi.

22. Quoted W.L. La Croix, *War and International Ethics: Tradition and Today* (Lanham: University Press of America, 1988), p. 63.

23. See Jonathan Riley-Smith, *What were the Crusades?* (Houndmills: Macmillan, 1977).
24. Note that Holy War is not to be contrasted with Just War in either case, since the former is taken to be a species of the latter.
25. This observation does not, however, apply to Aquinas, for whom a prince's authority does depend upon his obligations to uphold the common good of his people. See La Croix, *War and International Ethics*, p. 71.

2

The Right of Self-Defence

Defensive war

The only just cause for war allowed by defensive just war theory is, as I indicated in the previous chapter, self-defence. But what self-defence amounts to, in principle or in practice, is far from clear.[1] It is useful, however, to think of the collective conflicts which are in some sense more primitive than the institutionalised forms we refer to as wars. In these, one group of people attacks another, which has, just as an individual does, a right to defend itself. What the group is defending here, like the individual, is life, liberty, property or whatever, and their right of self-defence is an acknowledgement of the fact that people will, if possible, resist an attack which threatens these vital goals. An organised act of aggression by a state or analogous body upon another needs to be seen as an extension of such a collective conflict, and the attacked state's entitlement to fight as deriving from the very same right.

Unless we view matters in this light then we shall be obliged to see a state's right to defend itself, not as an example of people's right to defend their own lives and so on, but as merely analogous to this and as instantiating instead a state's defence of its territorial integrity and sovereignty. But this is a very unsatisfactory position for several reasons.[2] First, a person or group's right of self-defence in law allows them to kill an attacker so long as this is not directly intended and is their only method of defence. Yet it is quite unclear why territorial integrity and sovereignty should justify killing by analogy with this. Second, there will be cases where defending territory or sovereignty will involve citizens losing their lives or liberty rather than being defended, and it is unclear what is the basis in the analogy for this trade-off.

And third, it is not clear why actual aggression should be needed for a war to be defensive, since there are many threats to territorial integrity and sovereignty that do not involve aggression, for example, subversion, which would not be thought obviously to justify a war.

Instead, we need to link defence of territory and sovereignty to self-defence in a closer way than by mere analogy to defence of life and liberty. Rather, we need to see territorial integrity and political sovereignty as themselves expressions of the routine way in which people's lives and livelihoods are protected within states. It is the function of governments to provide for this by maintaining a system of law and order, within established borders and uncoerced by other agencies. While systems of legal control need not be territorial, in modern states they are, so that any threat to the borders of a territory is a threat to the maintenance of law and order as a means of protecting citizens. Similarly, coercion of a state's government risks it no longer acting to enforce the law to that end. If a state is attacked, then that threat to its territory and sovereignty is a potential threat to the lives and livelihoods of its citizens which have, we may suppose, enjoyed protection within it.

It is for this reason, I suggest, that the defence of territory and sovereignty themselves comes to be regarded as a just cause of war, even when it cannot be shown in a particular case that the lives and livelihoods of citizens are being directly defended. For within the international order there must be general rules and permissions designed to allow governments to perform their essential functions. Thus while some invasions may even be benign others will certainly not be. Not only is there no principled way of distinguishing them, but even in particular cases their effects on certain sections of a population may be impossible to predict. The deadly consequences for Jews, for example, of German advances in World War II could not easily have been foreseen. But these consequences flowed, for the most part, not from attacks *in* war, but from actions made possible *by* war, and which, unlike most attacks in war, successful defence could have averted.

The distinction is important and is one that is blurred by describing government as having responsibility for both external and internal security, as if the former simply protected citizens, through the armed forces, against violence from without as the latter protects them, through the legal system, against violence from within.[3] Yet what maintaining security principally does is preserve a social order in which personal safety can be protected, not directly protect that safety. The former task is directed as much against those forces that threaten the conditions of social order from within the borders of a state as against those that pose a threat from without. Self-defence as a possible recourse in the maintenance of security is, then, I am suggesting, the indirect defence of lives, liberty and livelihoods of citizens through the defence of the conditions which protect them. In what one might call the primitive case, however, direct and indirect defence merge into one, when a body of citizens confronts a rapacious attacker whose motives are to kill or enslave them and to despoil their lands.

That this case underlies international thinking about the right of self-defence is evident from the fact that the state is allowed to possess the right to protect its own citizens and not just its territory. How far this right extends to armed intervention abroad is a matter of legal debate,[4] but the existence of the right as what grounds the defensive use of force is undenied. In terrorist attacks, whether domestic or international, it is ordinary citizens who are put at risk and who require direct protection. Whether this is to be accomplished by the operation of the legal system or by military means is a question to which we shall return, but if it is by the latter then this is because, in the defensive version of just war theory, those attacks are regarded as acts against which the state needs to defend itself, just as if it were under attack, internally or internationally, by more conventional forces.

Proper authority

The account of self-defence that I have suggested indicates why it is that sub-state bodies, as well as states themselves, can validly claim to be acting in self-defence by taking up arms against the state they are in. There are again two sorts of circumstance in which they are justified in doing so. One is when the state itself is engaged in attacks against its own citizens which threaten their lives, liberty or livelihoods and these must be directly defended. The second is when the conditions for the protection of some or all citizens are threatened by the actions of the state. There are a variety of cases here, to which we shall return, but whereas in relations between states two conditions, namely territorial integrity and political sovereignty, are recognised as necessary, so that a threat to them is an indirect threat to a state's citizens which justifies defensive war, there are, in the internal situation, no such generally acknowledged conditions.

We must now turn, however, to a general objection to allowing that sub-state actors might take up arms against a state in a defensive just war. The first requirement of a just war in any version of the doctrine is that it is undertaken under the direction of a proper authority, which will normally be the duly constituted government of a state. On this criterion all wars undertaken by secessionists, for example, would fail to qualify as just. Indeed, it is at first sight hard to see how secessionists could even accept it as a requirement since they may take themselves to be fighting a just war even if their opponent is the government of the state. Their reply, of course, may be that this is not the government they ought to have and so it cannot itself claim to be a proper authority in opposing their political claims by force. There is a danger of confusion here, however, which we should first clear up. Proper authority to wage a war is a distinct notion from that of rightful authority to govern a certain territory. If they were not distinct, inter-state wars for control of such a territory would automatically involve one of the parties lacking authority to fight, namely the one which had no lawful authority to govern this territory whichever that was – which is precisely the point at issue between them. Yet this is not a conclusion we would wish to draw, preferring to base each side's authority to fight on its being a properly constituted state in the international order, whatever the justice of its particular territorial claims. So we must differentiate between the claim that a secessionist group has authority to fight and the claim that its state opponent lacks rightful authority to govern.

Here it is important to distinguish the way that authority to fight operates in modern defensive just war theory from its place in older doctrines. In its Christian origins the authority to fight was given to princes because they were supposed to derive their authority to administer justice from God, and war itself represented a means of delivering justice by punishing wrong doers. In the defensive theory, by contrast, authority to fight derives from being placed in a position to defend a territory and its people, for which a resort to war may be necessary, as explained in the previous section. Evidently it is the government of a state that will normally be put in this position, though there will be exceptions, as when a weak state operates under the protection of a stronger one pledged to defend it. It is from the needs of self-defence, then, that proper authority in war derives. But while this explains why authority to fight should be conceded to some person or body it does not explain what sort of a person or body that should be – what, in our preferred terminology, should be their role.

Authority to fight involves two aspects. One is that those who fight should be under effective control so that the rules of war, in particular those designed for the protection of civilians, should be observed. The danger of war is always that of unrestrained and passionate violence which only military discipline and, ultimately, political control can check. It is the duty of statesmen who possess the capacity to fight to ensure that this danger is not realised. States will normally have the means to do so through possessing a regular army with a chain of command answerable to the government for its actions. Arguably the government of a state whose armed forces operate to a greater or lesser extent outside of their control lacks authority to fight its internal opponents. Certainly such an army has no authority. For it is the government which is charged with the care of its civilian population and only it can be expected to have their interests at heart. Many conflicts in Africa and elsewhere illustrate the evils of uncontrolled armed forces and impotent governments. Even when the defence of a state's population against arbitrary attack is the aim of such a state it lacks the authority to achieve it by just means. In cases like this the only acceptable way to restore peace and order may be to invite in external assistance, though this risks internationalising the conflict in ways to which we shall have to return.

Do insurgents ever have an acceptable structure of authority to ensure the proper conduct of hostilities? Undoubtedly they often do not and anti-state rebels may violate the rules in part because of this, visiting their hostility upon civilians without any military purpose. But it is not obvious that insurgents *must* lack the structures which prevent this, either at the political or the military level. What, on the defensive theory, would tend to lend proper authority to insurgents would be their standing in a similar relation to a civilian population as an established and effective government. There is, in principle, no reason why they should not, though in practice there will be many obstacles in their way. One of these will be a proliferation of groups claiming to represent a section of the population, perhaps vying for supremacy and even resorting to violence in this internal struggle. For the right relation will require that this population looks to the group to defend it and to provide government, something that cannot be achieved if a number of groups are competing for their loyalty.

This brings us to the second aspect of proper authority, which is not independent of the first. For the reason why a proper authority must be able to control its forces is to ensure that their actions are applied to the purposes of the war and not otherwise. The second aspect of authority is that of being in a position to decide to go to war, that is to say, to determine whether one's purposes in doing so would be appropriate ones. On the defensive theory such purposes would need to serve the defence of some group of people. Unless a person is making decisions on these sorts of grounds she is not occupying the role of statesman or political leader in an appropriate way, but using the resources of the role for inappropriate purposes. Someone occupies the role in a way that confers authority, then, only if she stands in the right relation to the people she represents to make these decisions on their behalf and in what is taken to be their interest. This does not imply she needs a mandate from them.[5] People may not agree with the decision made by their leaders, but they must be able to trust their leaders to make the decisions for the right sort of reasons and with due regard to the consequences for them. Where there are no grounds for such trust, as when politicians go to war to enrich themselves for instance, for example in the Congo, then they lack proper authority.

Some go so far as to claim that force not used for identifiable political purposes is not war at all.[6] Certainly there is a problem, for example, of 'how to distinguish brigands and gangsters from genuine revolutionaries who merit moral and legal standing',[7] but it is better to look for an answer in terms of the kind of group that is involved rather than in the particular purposes they are engaged in. 'War', on this kind of account, 'is organised violence carried on by political units against each other'.[8] And what makes a unit political is its relation to other people – the fact that it acts in their name even if its leaders' purposes are self-interested and a betrayal of their trust. This allows us to see violence that has no identifiable political purposes as war even when it is 'blind, impulsive or habitual' – a fitting description for much that goes on in new wars as much as in the ritualistic tribal fighting of anthropological accounts.[9] Yet it still differs from the 'riots, isolated and sporadic acts of violence, and other acts of similar nature' denied the status of belligerency by international law, since this is not the behaviour of political units but of unorganised crowds or gangs.[10]

To be engaged in a war, however, political units must be of the right type. It is tempting to suggest they must be actual or potential governments with respect to a territory and its people. But this, though the typical case, would rule out groups like the Zapatistas of Mexico who simply wish to change policy vis-à-vis the peasants of the Chiapas, or Albanian insurgents in Macedonia who claim to pursue only cultural rights. It would also have ruled out sub-state wars between medieval barons who, although major political forces within their states, did not seek to govern in anything like the modern sense, but whose activities were precisely those that the just war requirement of proper authority was meant to curb. Perhaps we should rather say that the units involved in wars are political in the sense mentioned above of standing in a representative relation to others and that they are simply actual or political *powers* within a territory and over its people. Then war will be an armed contest for power, whatever purposes it is used for and whatever form it takes. On this sort of account proper authority will depend on the group's relation to people being of the right sort and its actual and potential power being of the right type and used for the right reasons.

What counts as having proper authority to fight is sometimes said to depend not upon a leader's relation to a community she represents but to her place in international society, to whose laws she subjects herself.[11] This is at first sight over restrictive in disqualifying non-state actors from having proper authority. But if we view the account as one that outlines what is required for someone to play the role of a leader charged with the defence of a group we can see that it gives her a determinate place vis-à-vis other leaders, whether of states or of sub-state groups, so that her behaviour is broadly predictable and accountable. If it were not then a range of relationships between statesmen of alliance, negotiation and so forth would be impossible. Yet normally the conduct of war is linked to such relationships which depend upon acknowledgement that the conditions for proper authority to fight are satisfied. We will turn next to see if these conditions might be fulfilled in new wars by noting that the just war doctrine that authority should rest with rulers admits of some exceptions.

Tyrannicide

In traditional just war theory it is sometimes allowed that subjects may, in exceptional circumstances, rebel against their ruler and even that an individual may act on their behalf to kill him. The circumstances are those in which the ruler has become a tyrant, oppressing his people rather then protecting them. In this situation he becomes like an external aggressor, and no more a lawful ruler than if he had wrongfully invaded the country. So long as the other conditions of just war are fulfilled, he may be deposed or killed by the use of armed force directed against him and his forces. The ruler himself loses the authority to fight which passes to the rebels or tyrannicide. Indeed on some versions of the theory it is tyrants themselves, who, by substituting force for law, are 'properly rebels' for it is they who defy authority.[12] But this is a quixotic usage. The rebels (in the customary sense) or tyrannicide represent people in the tyrant's stead 'on behalf of the community, in defence of values generally shared, against a tyranny generally recognised as such'.[13] Rebellion is prima facie preferable to tyrannicide since rebels will normally be drawn from the ranks of politicians who have a body of the public on their side and can be assumed to seek the public good, while there is a great risk that the individuals engaged in tyrannicide have their own private agenda rather than seeking exclusively to terminate a gross abuse of power and restore the *status quo ante* of jurisdictional rule.

What this line of thinking illustrates is the close connection that is made in just war theory between lawful authority to govern and authority to fight. The two are not, as I indicated earlier, synonymous. Yet whatever the other ingredients for having authority to govern may be, one is that such government should itself be, broadly speaking, just. That is to say it should be carried on by the administration of a fair system of law rather than by arbitrary or coercive actions. A tyrannical regime has departed from these requirements and forfeits authority in respect of those whom it oppresses. Similarly it loses authority to fight on their behalf, for such authority depends upon the presumption that the government will defend its people, a presumption that fails when its oppressive treatment of them itself amounts to an attack. There are questions of degree of oppression here, but we can safely say that where deadly force is employed against the people to bind them to a tyrant's will then this is tantamount to attack, and a tyrant lacks authority to resist by force the people's defence against him.

The connection between authority to fight and to govern is reflected in the conditions an armed group must fulfil to defend an oppressed population. It will have the right sort of relation to these people only if it acts in their interests to bring them, and continue to provide them with, peace and security, and can be recognised as doing this. Notice that this does not imply it must have 'legitimacy' in the sense that, for example, on a liberal theory, popular consent provides. What of this sort might be required is a further question and a contentious one. But it is one thing to act on behalf of a group of people in the way indicated, quite another to act on their behalf as of right, as the legitimacy requirement would demand. Rather, the sort of relation needed is one that goes along with the kind of power that a potential government would exercise and the purposes for which it would use it. As indicated earlier the kind of power involved must be constitutional power exercised through the administration of the law, rather than arbitrary or coercive power. Insofar as military power is needed to supplement this it must be used simply to secure a space within which jurisdiction can be maintained, which includes defence against external or internal aggression. The purposes for which power is used must be to further the interests of the people represented as a whole, not simply a section of them, still less the section from which the potential government is drawn. But it must be used within the bounds of inter-state relations, which prohibit, as we have seen, aggression against other groups.

Just war theory assumes, in its classic form, that in any particular state there is but a single community of people, so that if the government of the state becomes tyrannical then that is oppressive to all its people and demands a response from all of them.

Yet this is not at all the case in the sorts of situations which characterise many recent wars. What differentiates them from traditional revolutionary wars which can easily be fitted into the old wars picture is that they involve sectional insurgency. And the reason for this is very often the fact that only a particular section of the population of the state is, or feels itself to be, oppressed by the government. Thus the reason for the uprising in Kosovo was a sense that its ethnically Albanian majority was oppressed by a government acting in the interests of Serbs. The Timorese secession was similarly sparked by Indonesian governmental action, in this case very clearly oppressive to a minority. Examples could be multiplied. In all of them oppression is selective and the rest of the state's population is properly treated so that they have no grounds for complaint.

What we must ask about this sort of situation is whether it resembles that of classic just war theory in implying that the selectively oppressive government has lost its lawful authority to govern *throughout* the state. Arguably it has, if its title to authority depends upon its upholding the rights of people *qua* citizens. For then *qua* citizens none of its people has a good reason to obey its injunctions since these are not issued impartially and in accordance with law. Indeed that it treats only some of its subjects in this way makes its moral position worse rather than better, for it thereby reveals its partiality and failure to respect the rules for the proper performance of its governmental duties. The corollary of this view is that what is needed is a change of regime which will adopt a more enlightened approach, and this is exactly what outside observers often claim in situations where wars have broken out, identifying the selectively oppressive regime as lacking authority to govern in any of its territories and calling for its overthrow.

This picture is, I suggest, an over-simple one. Leaders may be able to play the role with respect to the people of their own country but not those of another, just as one may be able to fulfil the role of parent for one's own children but not those of others. Given this, we should not be surprised if leaders exercise partiality in regard to one section of their state's population, even to the extent of hostility to another. They are acting quite wrongly and have failed to perform their role in its required scope, just as a parent who favours one child and even mistreats others has done. But it does not follow that the leader has totally failed to perform her role, for she does perform it with respect to one section of the population.

Now, if this were just an isolated case of inappropriate behaviour by one person or group of people, a change of regime might well be the remedy. Yet this is unlikely to be the case in the sorts of situations we have in view. For the reason that such leaders come to power will probably be that they reflect the general sentiment of a dominant sector of the population and gain power because of this, just as Milosovicz rose to power through reflecting specifically Serbian feelings despite his duty to promote the interests of the whole of Yugoslavia. In these circumstances a government's selective oppression may attract, and indeed depend upon, the collusion of a dominant majority. It is doubtful whether, in that case, a mere change of regime will protect the oppressed minority. What may be needed is a constitutional change in which it is granted that within the structures of a single state they cannot be protected, and this is what secessionists claim.

We should not, therefore, take insurgents against selective oppression to be fighting impartially for the restoration of a status quo in which peoples' rights are not violated, as rebels act on the classic just war model. They are fighting for constitutional change and may have the authority to fight which derives from their defence of a section, rather than the whole, of the population. But by the same token we should not conclude that the government of the established state has forfeited authority globally. It retains it in the areas it administers with due regard to the law, and forfeits it elsewhere. It follows, however, that it retains the authority of a government to fight, so that a war of secession against an oppressive regime may have the character of an international conflict in that both sides have proper authority to fight.

Secession

Rebels waging a war of secession against an oppressive regime may not only have proper authority to fight, they may also satisfy the other conditions the theory imposes for having a right to fight. They may have the correct intention, viz. peace and security, and take up arms only as a last resort, with good hope of success and with no disproportionate ill effects. Lastly, but most importantly, they may have a just cause too, since on the defensive version of just war theory, self-defence is what provides such a cause. In the circumstances they are in, I have suggested, there may be no way for people to obtain a just peace short of seceding, so that secession is not some further objective, over and above self-defence. It is what needs to be achieved in order for them to defend themselves effectively. If only a separate state, or at the least an autonomous region, can protect them from very serious oppression then such a secession is something to which they have a right, just because they have a right to self-defence. Similar considerations could apply to other constitutional changes such as uniting with another state, if this were strictly required for their self-defence.

I shall term a right of secession that arises from these sorts of circumstances a 'circumstantial' right.[14] It is important to distinguish it very sharply from the right of secession that groups, particularly national groups, often claim, namely a 'systemic' right; that is to say, a right which derives not from the circumstances the group finds itself in but from the kind of group it is, for example a supposedly national group. Such a right, if it existed, would be systemic in that it would derive from a view about how a system of states might properly be devised, for example, a system in which there was a separate state for every nation (under some common characterisation of nationhood). A systemic right would derive from a group of the appropriate kind having a right of self-determination. I shall, in Chapter 3, examine this alleged right since it is, of course, characteristic of many new wars that they originate in such a claim made by a national or other group, and denied by the established state. Here, though, it is important to see that self-defence and national self-determination are quite different grounds for justifying secession.

This is a point that is easily overlooked since separatist groups are often fighting for both causes. Indeed there is often a connection between the people they represent being oppressed and a separate state being claimed for them as a particular kind of group. This can work in both directions. In one, a section of a state's population may be discriminated against and worse because they are categorised as different in a way that supposedly justifies inferior treatment. Categorisation of this kind may lead to group identification of a sort and strength that was not previously present. Discrimination may produce a shared sense of common predicament and a consequential group solidarity. These are the ingredients of national consciousness, or something analogous, and its resulting demand for self-determination. Something like this seems to have happened in Yugoslavia, where people who had previously thought of themselves simply as Yugoslavs were forced into identifying as Croats, Serbs, Bosnian Muslims and so forth as they found themselves so categorised and discriminated against by their neighbours. This had the result that originally small scale nationalisms grew in strength, with different groups who found themselves oppressed in different parts of the country making common cause with their fellows who were elsewhere in a majority – people with whom they had little in common.

In the other direction, oppression can result in an obvious way from the development of group self-identification, especially when this is linked to demands for self-determination. For this may be taken to threaten the unity and even the territorial integrity of the state. Oppressive measures may be taken against the group either by way of reactions of resentment at and denial of their claimed status, or as a deliberate instrument of policy in suppressing revolt. For our present purposes, however, we must distinguish those forms of oppression which are aimed at assimilation and thus the suppression of people's self-identification as a separate group, at least for political purposes; and those directed at exclusion, which accept this group identity but seek to exclude members of the group, either from political participation or from the state altogether, the limiting case of which is genocide. The former sort of case is illustrated by Turkey's present treatment of the Kurds – or 'Mountain Turks', as it prefers to call them in refusing to acknowledge their separate identity; the latter by its historic treatment of Armenians, who, perhaps because of their separate faith, seem to have been deemed unassimilable. While the latter kind of treatment can clearly involve far worse atrocities than are consistent with the former, both can give rise to oppression serious enough for people to have to defend themselves in order to live a tolerable life.

Where the borderline is crossed between degrees of oppression that do not justify an armed response and those that do is a difficult question. But it is important to see the kind of defence against tyrannical governments which just war theory allows: one that protects *individuals* against physical attack or, arguably, other grave violations of their rights, such as forcible relocation, break up of families, deprivation of livelihood and so forth. It is not an attack on them *as a group* that they are to be defended from, on a defensive understanding of just war theory, for their existence as a separate group is not itself something to which people have a right simply as citizens of a state, and it is a violation of their rights as citizens that justifies rebellion. Rather their existence as a separate group is the consideration that is invoked in a struggle for national self-determination, not for self-defence. It is easy to confuse these causes, however, when people are oppressed *qua* members of some group. Then it is likely both that they will be subjected to harm as individuals and that the cultural institutions and practices which knit them together as a group – their church, language or whatever – will come under attack.

When a group does resort to force to press its claim for self-determination then it is very likely indeed that the established state will proceed against not only its combat units, but also against the civilian population from which they are drawn and which is seen as harbouring them. Doubtless too, the state will maintain that it is simply doing what is needed to suppress rebellion and restore jurisdictional rule throughout its territories. Here, I would argue, a situation can arise in which, without possessing at the outset the just cause of defending people against oppression, insurgents can come to have one, precisely because the response of the established state offends the rules of war and puts people in the position of needing to be defended by the rebels. The state will claim that it is directing force against the minority *qua* rebels, which it has, within limits, a right to do. But if it appears that in fact particular violence is being directed against them *qua* members of the group then this claim will be suspect. Although it may be hard to judge where the truth lies a history of discrimination short of oppression may tilt the scales against the state's story. Even where there is not, some measures are so disproportionate to the military situation and so indiscriminate in their effects on civilians that they can only be interpreted as directed against the minority per se, not against it as a rebellious group. In this sort of situation the rebels gain a justification which they did not previously possess.

The lesson for states is that they should not be provoked in this way, even if the tactics of separatist rebels are designed to elicit such a reaction. They must continue to treat rebellious subjects as citizens on equal terms with others, even if they would prefer not to remain so, and this implies having an even greater regard for their well-being than is strictly required by the laws of war. For to do otherwise plays into the hands of those who demand to be treated as a distinct group precisely by so treating them. This is the trap into which, it has been suggested, the federal Yugoslav government fell through forcing ethnic Albanian civilians to leave as a response to the Kosovo Liberation Army insurgency, though the situation was a complex one with semi-autonomous irregular forces operating on both sides and bombing by external states creating fear. In this sort of situation it is the agents of the state who step outside the requirements of their roles to carry forward by force the politics of identity. Conversely, the rebels, while starting forth from an identity politics, can, through fighting to defend their people, acquire a recognised role. But such a role imposes, as we have continually stressed, stringent requirements. Even if rebels have a just cause they need, as I indicated earlier, proper authority, and this they lack unless they are prepared to be bound by the requirements of the role. Identity politicians and their forces may well not be, instead treating the enemy as they have been treated by them.

Wars of secession may then be, but probably will not be, old wars rather than new, in that they may be fought between the established state on the one hand and separatists on the other, both of whom are acting from a perception of the interests of the citizens they represent. Politicians may act inappropriately without their performance of their role being distorted by considerations of identity. Failure to respect the requirements of the role may stem from other sources. In the case of those representing the established state, their resort to oppression of a minority may originate in a misplaced view that the state's interests override the constraints of constitutional rule. In the case of those representing the minority, they may seek a separation not to end any oppression but simply to advance a sectional interest, but again pursuit of such an interest beyond the constitutional constraints is an abuse of power. Armed forces too can behave badly for reasons quite other than the passions of identity politics. So long as we have conflicts in which the actors retain their roles, even if they flout their requirements, we do not yet have the sort of phenomena characteristic of new wars. And, importantly, they can still be held to account for their conduct by reference to the role requirements of statesmen and soldiers in old wars. In new wars such standards tend simply to lose their application.

Jihad

I want to illustrate this discussion of the possibility of a just war fought by sub-state actors in self-defence by considering a deeply problematic case. On 11 September 2001 the world was shocked by the hijacking of four US passenger planes, two of which were crashed into the twin towers of the World Trade Center in New York, with huge civilian casualties, and another into the Pentagon, the fourth hitting the ground with the loss of all aboard after passengers overpowered the hijackers. There is no doubt but that these acts were gross violations of the rules of war. Yet on the reasonable assumption that they were intended as acts of war against the US could the waging of such a war by sub-state actors possibly be justified? Could they, in other words, possess *jus ad bellum*?

Such questions may seem shocking, but they need to be se-riously addressed since the presumed perpetrators of the out-rage appear to claim such a case, if not for this action then for analogous ones. Such actions are carried out by Islamic revolu-tionary organisations on the grounds that the US is engaged in actions which are oppressive to Muslims, for example through the bombing of and economic sanctions upon Iraq, and gives material support to other states engaged in such actions, in par-ticular to Israel in its occupation of Palestinian territory. Islamic organisations claim to be acting in defence of Muslims who are being oppressed.[15] They would satisfy the condition of having a just cause if those on whose behalf they were fighting – the Palestinians, say – were unlawfully oppressed in the way that is claimed, and others could acquire a just cause through allying with them. For they are not, on any ordinary construction, them-selves acting in self-defence, as some Palestinians take themselves to be acting in launching attacks on Israel or Israelis. The cru-cial question becomes, therefore, whether the organisations have proper authority to wage war and whether they have the right intention. For we may suppose, for the sake of argument, that they believe the other conditions are satisfied, namely that their war is a last resort, proportionate in its costs to the further op-pression which, in addition, it has a good chance of preventing; though all these are, of course, highly contentious matters.

It is fairly evident that the Islamic organisations that launch attacks against the US are not themselves governmental organisations even if they are harboured and even to some degree sponsored by states. If they were then we would have a case where they were the sort of body that would have authority to fight and the only question that would arise is whether they have authority to fight in this cause, which, I suggest, they would possess only if they allied with those with a right of self-defence – a matter to which I shall return in a later chapter. But if they are not governmental organisations nor organisations of those who feel themselves oppressed and set out to change their conditions to prevent it – in the Palestinian case, for instance, attempting to form a state – then what is the nature of their claim to represent oppressed people?

On the face of it the claim seems quite groundless. It is not at all obviously in the interests of those who are allegedly defended that these actions against the US are taken; and those people may well be able to recognise this and consequently not be able to place their trust in the Islamic organisations who take them. Indeed, they show no particular interest in securing such trust and would seemingly continue their campaign without it. Furthermore, they might even be prepared to sacrifice the interests of those supposedly defended for some larger end, an indication of their unfitness to represent them. Nor is it clear that the power they might gain were they so recognised would be limited to constitutional applications in the interests of the governed. By these tests for authority Islamic revolutionary organisations are found wanting. They do not act in a way that suggests that people could put faith in them to judge whether and how to fight in war on their behalf.

The reason for this is, as we have in fact already noticed, that their intentions in waging war are not limited to the defence of those directly harmed and the bringing of a just peace to them. We need to be careful here, however, not to condemn those fighting a war simply because they have additional intentions to those that might justify it. Thus it was no good argument against the IRA to say they were fighting for a united Ireland when their immediate aim was the defence of Catholics against attacks launched upon them by Protestants.[16] What determines whether the relevant intention is appropriate is whether the actions it governs are of a sort that can normally be taken to defend people and ultimately provide them with security, rather than exposing them to further danger in pursuit of another goal. By this criterion, as I indicated, the militant Islamists seem to fail. Indeed, their tactics of suicidal attack, justified as martyrdom, strongly suggest that their further ends quite outweigh the protection of individual lives which is the essence of defence.

The problem with these conclusions is that they do not seem to touch the Islamic revolutionaries' own conception of what gives them authority to fight and what makes their intentions the right ones; and this raises questions, of course, about the applicability of just war theory across cultural boundaries. Authority is claimed on the grounds that Muslims have a duty of *jihad*, which includes the defence of fellow Muslims. Anyone acting to defend his fellows in this way would be acting with authority, and the source of such authority is the will of Allah as revealed in the Koran. In fact the assumption is that Muslims will manifest such solidarity that an attack on one counts as an attack on all, so that such defence is actually a form of self-defence. But the purpose of this is the strengthening of Islam itself, so that building unity among Muslims is just another aspect of *jihad*.

All this, on the face of it, seems to open the way to all the dangers of private war that the requirement of proper authority is intended to avert, and in the proliferation of Islamic armed groups with their varying strategies and tactics that is just what we have been witnessing. Yet why should the Koranic injunctions of solidarity and self-defence necessarily lead to that? There seems no reason in principle why the duty of defence of oppressed Muslims should not be assumed by predominantly Muslim states, allying with those who defend themselves against oppression. Though this sometimes raises difficult questions about the ethics of intervention in the internal affairs of other countries, to which we shall return in Chapter 6, it at least takes these conflicts out of the uncontrollable area of private war. For where states are involved negotiation and arbitration are always possibilities that have to be exhausted before resort to war. Nor is there anything novel about such alliances, for throughout the nineteenth century Christian governments acted in the defence of those Christian subjects of the Ottoman Empire whom they saw to be oppressed. It is a relevant and perhaps inescapable fact of international relations that such selective assistance is offered. There is nothing specific to the culture of Islam involved in it.

Such action is, of course, a manifestation of the politics of identity, in this instance the shared identity of Muslims, though in the kind of cases just mentioned this was mediated through the politics of role and thereby kept in check by the application of international norms. What such mediation achieves is the interposition of structures of authority that are not themselves based on identity. Thus the Islamic groups' claim to have authority simply in virtue of sharing an identity and for that reason alone being able to act on behalf of co-religionists is denied. For what this would assume is a tacit unity of purpose and even an agreement as to means – an assumption, characteristic of militant identity politics, which sucks those of the given identity into courses of action decided by small groups.

This brings us to the issue of the militant Islamists' intentions in waging campaigns of terror. That intention is, it would seem, principally the Pan-Islamist one of bringing all Muslims under a common governance within a shared state. This has sometimes been construed as opposing religion as a foundation of statehood to national identity. But it is perhaps better to view it as a conflict between different nationalisms. As one commentator writes: 'Under the traditions and unwritten rules of Islam there can be no such thing as an individual and sovereign Islamic nation set apart from the rest of Islam, all Islam is a single nation.'[17] This places the intentions of Islamic militants firmly in the same tradition as Western nationalisms in seeking a statehood based upon a certain kind of common national identity. Theirs may be, therefore, as we shall go on to investigate in the next chapter, a reasonable political ambition. But it is not an ambition that yields a just cause under defensive just war theory. Yet whether it does provide a good reason to fight depends upon beliefs that are not at all culturally alien to us.

The state's response

What, though, of a state's response to violence from sub-state actors: does it not have a duty to protect its citizens, especially from direct attacks by such forces? For example, is not America acting in self-defence in the War on Terror, following the September 11 atrocities, contrary to my characterisation of the war in Chapter 1? There are, as I mentioned earlier and will pursue later, many questions about how the undoubted duty of a state to protect its citizens should be discharged: military strikes against attackers are but one recourse. Yet, are they not sometimes an appropriately defensive one? This cannot be doubted, but it is important to try to spell out what the character of such a defensive response should be, and to compare it with other sorts of response which cannot be viewed as purely defensive.

The point, as I have stressed, of self-defence is to protect lives, liberties and livelihoods either directly or indirectly. The intention is to restore a situation of peace in which all citizens can lead secure and orderly lives. The task of statesmen is to carry out policies which will have these consequences for their own citizens while recognising that their fellow statesmen elsewhere have the same responsibilities. It is crucial, therefore, that a military reaction be an effective means to these ends, embarked upon when all others have been found ineffective; and proportionate to the attack, in the sense that it does not cause more harm than is strictly necessary to the proper ends of reacting to it. While anything one concludes about the policies for reacting to attacks adopted by particular states or combinations of states at particular times is inevitably controversial, it is only by measuring them against these yardsticks that judgements can be reached and, indeed, the nature of the yardsticks themselves be clearly revealed.

What we must ask, therefore, about the War on Terror is, firstly, whether it is a last resort. In particular we need to ask whether, on the one hand, non-military methods of achieving security for Americans might be equally effective and, on the other, whether diplomatic methods, including those which address any legitimate concerns that the Islamists might have, might equally have reduced the threat from them and sapped their support. No doubt policies of this sort would have incurred costs for an administration which adopted them, in particular that of appearing weak, of giving in to violence and of failing to reassure anxious citizens. But any genuine risks to security here must be carefully distinguished from damage to the political fortunes of a particular government, and it is of the essence of statesmanship to be able to make such distinctions and to be motivated only by the former considerations. It is, at best, unclear whether the War on Terror was waged as a last resort in respect of defence, or whether, which is quite a different matter, it was a last resort in respect of the aim of bringing those who attacked the US to justice.

Next, we should consider whether the war is a proportionate response. Here we are not concerned simply with whether the various campaigns in the war have or will cost more lives than were lost in the terrorist attacks, for such an application of the *lex talionis* is quite irrelevant to a war's defensive purposes.[18] Rather we are concerned with whether or not the costs of the war to all parties are outweighed by its defensive benefits. Notice that the costs to all parties must be weighed up, for, although the duty of a statesman is to his own citizens, he must be mindful of the consequences of his acts for others, since his fellow statesman have analogous duties. It is not acceptable, then, to wage a defensive war at the price of exposing other states to much greater insecurity, unless, perhaps, such a war is the only means of preventing some quite catastrophic consequences for one's own state.

There are no *a priori* criteria for determining what is permissible here. This is, to a large extent, determined by the reactions of other states to a particular policy, proposed or put into effect, and these are expressed either through diplomatic channels or through military operations themselves. Thus it is arguable that the War on Terror, as an ostensible defence of Western interests, has destabilised many predominantly Muslim states with potentially disastrous consequences. Whether such effects actually are disproportionate is also a moot point, but it is a point that Western statesmen need to consider. This is not to say, however, that it is up to them to determine what is in the interests of people generally. Statesmen should properly pursue the interests of their own states for that is their role, but in doing so they must avoid certain kinds of consequence for other states, which is also determined by their role. It is questionable whether Western statesmen, with their vision for the world order, have limited themselves appropriately in performing their roles; or whether they have discounted the short-term effects of the War on Terror under the millenarian influence of that vision.

The last requirement to consider is effectiveness: there must be a reasonable prospect that the war be successful in its aim of defending citizens directly or indirectly. Here it is crucial that the stated objectives of the war can be shown to serve this ultimate aim. The problem with the War on Terror is that its objectives seem too ambitious to be achievable. That terrorism should be eliminated everywhere and for all time as an instrument of resistance seems scarcely likely; nor is it necessary for a reasonable level of self-defence, any more than the elimination of all crime within a state is needed, or attainable, for a tolerable level of personal security. The difference between the cases, though, is important, for, whereas for there to be a system of law and order there must be the regular application of sanctions for breaches of the law wherever possible, irrespective of their particular effects in achieving personal security for citizens, defence against attack by military means is a purely pragmatic reaction, not part of a settled procedure, either for regulating relations between states or for dealing with insurgencies within them.

It follows from this last point that the effectiveness of a war in terms of self-defence must be carefully distinguished from its expressive purpose in registering indignation at a wrong. If the War on Terror, like many more limited campaigns against terrorism, is a war of reprisal against attackers then it may well fall into the latter category. If so then it will be a punitive rather than a defensive war, and as such unjustified in international law and the sort of ethics upon which this is based. Statesmen who authorise such a war will doubtless be reflecting their citizens' reactions, but they will be acting outside their more limited role of protecting those citizens. The criterion of effectiveness for such a punitive campaign is not its success in restoring peace and security, but in visiting retribution upon attackers and their sympathisers whether or not this changes their behaviour.

The justification of reprisals against terrorism which is often offered as an argument for their defensive purpose is that they are a deterrent, not only to potential attackers but to states which would harbour them and people who would offer support. The difficulty with this kind of argument is that it rests upon purely empirical foundations, which need to be substantiated in any particular case. It is a mere matter of fact whether reprisals do deter in the suggested manner, or whether they produce corresponding outrage that recruits more to a cause and increases its support. This is not something that can be settled *a priori* nor does it seem to be susceptible of any easy generalisations: sometimes reprisals have the one effect, sometimes the other. If this is the case, however, reprisals as ostensibly defensive cannot simultaneously be regarded as the visiting of retribution upon wrongdoers as part of an attempt to enforce certain international standards of behaviour. To the extent that the War on Terror has this as an explicit purpose, and in the absence of empirical evidence of its deterrent effect, it cannot, it may be suggested, be regarded as a defensive war.

Notes

1. For a good discussion to which I am indebted see Suzanne Uniacke, 'Self-Defence and Just War', in D. Janssen & M. Quante (eds), *Gerechter Krieg* (Paderborn: Mentis-Verlag, 2002).
2. *Pace* Michael Walzer, *Just and Unjust Wars* (New York: Basic, 1992).
3. Cp. D.D. Raphael, *Problems of Political Philosophy* (London: Macmillan, 1976), p. 46.
4. See Christine Gray, *International Law and the Use of Force* (Oxford: Oxford University Press, 2000), pp. 108–11.
5. *Pace* William V. O'Brien, *Law and Morality in Israel's War with the PLO* (New York: Routledge, 1991), p. 290.
6. E.g. D.P. Lackey, *The Ethics of War and Peace* (Eaglewood Cliffs: Prentice Hall, 1989), p. 30. I made the same mistake in my *Terrorism, Security and Nationalism* (London: Routledge, 1994), p. 30.
7. W.L. La Croix, *War and International Ethics* (Lanham: University Press of America, 1988), p. 256.
8. Hedley Bull, *The Anarchical Society* (Houndmills: Macmillan, 1977), p. 84.
9. Ibid., p. 186.
10. Geneva Convention 1977, Protocol 1, Articles 1–2, quoted Lackey, *The Ethics of War and Peace*.
11. Cp. A.L. Coates, *The Ethics of War* (Manchester: Manchester University Press, 1997), pp. 126–8.
12. John Locke, *Second Treatise of Civil Government* (many editions, 1690), sect. 226.
13. O. Jaszi & J.D. Lewis, *Against the Tyrant* (Glencoe: Free Press, 1957), p. 91.
14. Cp. Allen Buchanan, *Secession* (Boulder: Westview, 1991), pp. 27–81.
15. See the statement by Bin Laden cited ch. 1, fn. 8.
16. See my 'Just War: Theory and Application', *Journal of Applied Philosophy* 4, 1987.
17. Thomas Kiernan, *The Arabs* (London: Sphere, 1975), p. 200.
18. *Lex talionis*: the principle of an eye for an eye.

3

Myths of Identity

Tribalism

> In the first years of the 1990s, the old enmities and rivalries that were frozen for half a century in the Cold War glacier have come to life...After a hibernation of fifty years, the interethnic and intertribal tensions of Eastern Europe are awake once again. These regional conflicts have produced chaos, instability, bloodshed, and new powerful warlords to such a degree that they are found unacceptable in the West.[1]

Thus does an American political scientist express a common view of the cause of at least very many new wars. The kind of group identification that makes new wars possible is sometimes described as a 'resurrection of tribalism' in which supposedly primitive and irrational instincts engendering intergroup hatred and violence displace the modern, rational dispositions towards social co-operation and harmony which are fostered by most contemporary states.[2] This so-called 'dark gods' theory of identity politics, such as nationalism, is one that sees new wars as needing no special explanation once the constraints enforced by well-functioning states have been removed, as in the dissolution of the Soviet Union and Yugoslavia, and the collapse of central authority in many parts of Africa.[3] Tribal loyalties and enmities are, it is supposed, a natural fact of human life, to be held in check but not removed, so that, in Francis Bacon's words: 'Upon the shivering and breaking of a great State and Empire you may be sure to have wars.'[4]

In considering this explanation of new wars I turn to the account of collective identity provided by Sigmund Freud. It is a theory aspects of which have been alluded to in recent semi-popular accounts of the resurgence of nationalist conflict in the

post-Cold War world. Thus Michael Ignatieff has appealed to
Freud to characterise the war between Serbs and Croats. 'An out-
sider is struck,' he writes, 'not by the differences between Serbs
and Croats, but by how similar they seem to be.' But 'Freud,' he
notes, 'once argued that the smaller the real difference between
two peoples the larger it was bound to loom in their imagina-
tions. He called this effect the narcissism of minor difference. Its
corollary must be,' Ignatieff continues:

> that enemies need each other to remind themselves of who they really
> are. A Croat, thus, is someone who is not a Serb. A Serb is someone
> who is not a Croat. Without hatred of the other, there would be no
> clearly defined national self to worship and adore.[5]

In a subsequent volume Ignatieff devotes a chapter to developing this theme. In it he quotes a passage from Freud's
'Civilisation and its Discontents': 'It is always possible to bind
together a considerable number of people in love, so long as
there are other people left over to receive the manifestations of
their aggressiveness.'[6] It is the same passage as that quoted by
a commentator writing in a similar vein to Ignatieff, William
Pfaff, in a book whose title – *The Wrath of Nations: Civilisation
and the Furies of Nationalism* – adequately conveys its theme.
'Nationalism,' continues Pfaff, 'does not need complicated expla-
nations. Its links to the primordial human attachments to family,
clan, and community seem obvious.'[7] What, though, is Freud's
theory like, and what implications does it actually have for our
conception of nationalism and the like?

Freud derives his account of group formation from two processes in the individual. The first process is the subject's taking
from others an 'ego-ideal' on which to model her conduct and
upon which to direct her narcissistic feelings. In this process the
object of admiration who provides the ideal is 'introjected' into
the self, enriching it, as Freud expresses the matter.[8] This is illustrated in the individual case by identification with an admired
person. Freud uses this introjective process to explain group formation by suggesting that what binds the members together is
that they 'have put one and the same object in the place of their
ego-ideal and have consequently identified with one another in
their ego'.[9] There is, as one may put it, both a vertical and a horizontal bond.[10] The vertical bond links each member to the same
object as providing their ego-ideal. This may be a charismatic

leader, or, in his absence, some idea that takes his place. The leader or leading idea, Freud suggests, might also be 'negative', so that 'hatred...might operate in just the same unifying way, and might call up the same kind of emotional ties as positive attachment'.[11] But in the usual case the vertical ties will be clearly libidinal, as will the horizontal ones.

In these ties between group members, Freud explains, 'Love instincts which have been diverted from their original aims' are drawn upon to establish identification with those who share the same ego-ideal; and because they are aim inhibited the ties they create are lasting ones.[12] 'If I love someone,' Freud says elsewhere:

> he must deserve it in some way...He deserves it if he is so like me in important ways that I can love myself in him; and he deserves it if he is so much more perfect than myself that I can love my ideal of my own self in him.

But failing that, as one who is not a member of the group will fail, 'it will be hard for me to love him'.[13]

On the face of it the introjective process described here seems sufficient to provide an explanation of how groups are formed and maintained in terms of their members' individual psychologies. It explains, for example, a phenomenon to which Ignatieff draws attention, namely that though 'modernity...has been steadily reducing the differences between [Serbs and Croats]. Nonetheless, nationalism has turned the imagined differences into an abyss.'[14] For, as Freud observes, panic can arise 'owing to the disappearance of the emotional ties which hold the group together',[15] and against this the group will set up a fierce resistance by exaggerating those differentiating features upon which group ties depend. Yet, as we noticed, Ignatieff connects this with what Freud terms the 'narcissism of minor differences': 'The Englishman casts every kind of aspersion upon the Scot, the Spaniard despises the Portuguese,' and so on.[16] But, in his own work, Freud links this effect to a different process involved in group formation.

This second process in the individual is the projection of repressed impulses upon other people. In particular, it is aggressive feelings which are projected onto others, thus serving to rationalise their expression in oneself. For, Freud observes, in every human relationship feelings of hostility vie with those of fellowship. When a group is formed, however, aversion to-wards other members is displaced by love, and transferred to outsiders – those who are 'left over to receive the manifestations of... aggressiveness' – so that the group members may be bound together by the libidinous impulses which Freud distinguishes categorically from the aggressive ones. Any difference, however minor, may be drawn upon to construct an in-group and an out-group (though it is going too far to assert, with Ignatieff, that 'it is precisely because the differences... are minor that they must be expressed aggressively').[17] Any difference can be drawn upon because, Freud claims, narcissism 'behaves as though any diver-gence from his own particular lines of development involved a criticism', and is therefore to be aggressively resisted.[18]

It is, as I said, not quite clear whether Freud regards this second projective process as needed for group formation in addition to the first introjective one, though it is evident that he regards them as complementary and mutually supportive. The question is not a purely academic one. For if we reject – as we should – Freud's view of aggression as an elementary, instinctual drive then the accounts of nationalism by writers who draw on this aspect of his work, like Ignatieff and Pfaff, lose their appeal: a nationalist conflict is not profitably to be thought of as a resurgence of pri-mal hostilities when unchecked by the controls of a Hobbesian state.[19,20]

What other consequences does Freud's theory of group psy-chology yield for an account of national and ethnic identi-ties? To take an issue keenly debated by contemporary theo-rists of nationalism, does Freud's theory imply a primordialist account of nations, as Pfaff for one supposes, or is it, as Ignatieff thinks, compatible with modernism? What do these terms mean? Clifford Geertz, who may be credited with initiating the debate, explains that:

> By a primordial attachment is meant one that stems from the 'givens' – or, more precisely... the assumed 'givens' of social exis-tence: immediate contiguity and kin connection mainly, but beyond them... being born into a particular religious community, speaking a particular language... and following particular social practices.[21]

This idea is taken up by Walker Connor who contrasts such 'subconscious and emotional' attachments with 'conscious and rational' ones, calling Freud to the aid of the claim that 'national identity defied articulation in rational terms' by citing Freud's sense of being bonded to other Jews by 'many obscure and emotional forces, which were the more powerful the less they could be expressed in words, as well as by a clear consciousness of inner identity, a deep realisation of sharing the same psychic structure'.[22] This Connor glosses as expressing the same sentiment as the German maxim *Blut will zu Blut!* – a clear expression of a particular species of primordialism.

It should be apparent from the foregoing account, however, that there is nothing in Freud's theory to support this, or indeed any other kind of primordialism based upon ethnic affinities, however characterised. Freud's theory is quite general: it applies to any kind of group and imposes no restrictions on the sorts of affinity which may relate its members. This has implications for a view that Ignatieff and Pfaff both share, in common with many others, namely that there is something fundamentally different between *ethnic* nationalism, which is thought of as dangerous and passional and, on the other hand, *civic* nationalism, which is regarded as safe and rational. Whatever the truth in this contrast,[23] nothing in Freud's theory provides any justification for it. Precisely the same passions of love and hatred can be expressed in each, and neither is, in terms of its principles of formation, more or less 'rational' than the other. Or rather, for here we need to be more precise than theorists of nationalism often are, the principles that govern the members' attachment to a group are to be explained similarly in both cases, for it is this that Freud's theory seeks to explain.

It should then be evident that Freud's theory is, as Ignatieff rightly divines and Pfaff wrongly denies, compatible with modernism, if we understand by this the doctrine that nations are a specifically modern type of group formation. For the theory tells us nothing about what types of group there will be, only about the principles that ensure their cohesiveness. Quite a different type of explanation will be required to account for the types of group that arise in different socio-historical circumstances. This may, to take up Walker Connor's emotional/rational contrast, explain nation formation as a rational response to these circumstances, in the sense that it serves the interests of group members, or at least the interests of some privileged subset of them; or it may explain nation formation, as Connor would claim, non-rationally, in terms, for example, of a falling back on kinship ties in the face of modern uncertainties. But none of that would follow from the passional character of individual members' attachment to their nation, which Connor encapsulates in the observation 'people do not voluntarily die for things that are rational'.[24]

The defence of nationality?

Ulster Unionists claim that they just *do* feel loyalty to their fellow Britons and not to the Irish in the South of Ireland who disavow that loyalty. Had the country not been partitioned, their objection to the state's demands for their allegiance would have been that their allegiance just *was* differently directed, in the same way that Roger Casement, on trial for treason following the Easter Rising, asserted that: 'Loyalty is a sentiment, not a law. It rests on love, not on restraint.'[25] Loyalty, that is to say, cannot be commanded by a state, where it is not already felt – a view echoed by Irish Nationalists in Northern Ireland now. Thus, it is alleged, if these are the sorts of sentiments that people do feel then any view about what political obligations people owe which ignores this fact will founder, as people will lack the motivation necessary to discharge such obligations. What they are, in fact, motivated to discharge are *national* obligations, and it is upon such motivations that effective states must draw.

How should we assess such an appeal to the supposed facts of national allegiance? It would be unfair to assume that it treats national sentiment as simply a primordial feature of human life, in the manner of the 'dark gods' theory. The claim is that attachment to nations are *given*, not that they are *natural*, which would constitute only one possible explanation of their being given. Nor would this be a plausible explanation, even if the problem of the relative modernity of nations could be overcome by some such device as supposing that they replace earlier forms of social organisation while embodying the features that make them the focus of allegiance. There are a host of other reasons to explain why we might co-operate with those who share our supposed national identity, including the fact that it is just much easier to do so, and thus the naturalist explanation looks redundant.

Those who claim that we must start from national sentiments that are given need no naturalist underpinnings, nor need they ostensibly embrace ethnic rather than civic nationalism. Indeed the most prominent present exponent of this sort of position, David Miller, adopts a version of the latter, albeit eschewing the label 'nationalism', and is at pains to distinguish nationality from ethnicity. He finds, however, an important affinity: 'Like nations, ethnic groups tend to think of themselves as extended families... there is also often a sense of a family home.'[26] 'It is,' as another commentator remarks, 'a familiar feature of the rhetoric of nationalism that it evokes the language of family and kin relationships',[27] so it is important to establish what role this imagery plays. Miller not only reports it but adopts it, in arguing for an analogy between special obligations to family members and those to co-nationals. It is not just that we find ourselves accepting or discharging family obligations. It is that we attach a value to doing so because the relationships involved in the exchange of such obligations are of deep significance in our lives and they have this significance because they make us who we are – the son or daughter of such and such a person, husband or wife of another, and so on. Do national obligations arise from our identities in just this sort of way?

It is important to see that the model of the nation as a family does not depend upon the idea that the relationships within it are natural ones arising from common kinship, despite the fact that its most influential exponent, Herder, made just this assimilation by declaring that: 'A people is a natural growth, like a family, only spread more widely.'[28] The family model regards members of a nation as bound together into a certain sort of community. Membership of such a community generates an identity, rather than just a limited role, for, as in the family itself, so in the national community I enter a network of relationships – normally involuntarily – whose obligations are wide-ranging and indeterminate. The national community's goals and demands are, other things being equal, made my own. As in the family, the fact that my identity is shaped by membership gives me a reason to fulfil the obligations of membership, and I will value the sort of relationship that this exchange of obligation brings.

The question that immediately arises, of course, is whether I will be right to do so. The issue is not whether mutual trust, solidarity and so on are not really good things in themselves, but whether they are to be valued in the form and context of a national community as, we are supposing at least for the sake of argument, that they are good within the family. To answer this question Miller must fall back – with David Hume – on the broad assumption that: 'the generosity of man is very limited, and that it seldom extends . . . at most, beyond their native country'.[29] The family is, however, an inherently dangerous image for the defenders of nationalism to deploy. For though we can distinguish analytically between its use to ground national obligations in communities and its use to derive them from kinship, there is a natural and perhaps inevitable slide from the former to the latter and thus from a possibly civic to an inescapably ethnic nationalism.

Yet it is one thing to model nations on families, quite another to explain the fact that people do have special obligations to particular groups of people by analogy with their family duties. A politics of role, by contrast with a politics of identity, is in fact quite compatible with a particularist story of special obligations to fellow citizens which do not depend upon sentiments that are simply given. Consider, for example, the demands of parenthood that are keenly felt by the vast majority of those who experience it. These need not be regarded as the result of instinctive urges mysterious to us, but as a consequence of our grasping the ethical responsibilities of our role because we understand its function and therefore seek to discharge its responsibilities conscientiously. They do, of course, involve treating our own children preferentially in a multitude of ways over those of other people, but in ways that are, in fact, strictly prescribed and by no means as open-ended as a communal account might suggest they would be, for there can be no principled limits on the promptings of natural urges. We must do what we can to help our children, but not in ways that deliberately disadvantage those of others. Nor, of course, are such prescriptions limited to our natural children, they apply to any to whom we stand in the parental role.

This is but a sketchy indication of the way a delineation of roles can account for the ethical particularism involved in family relationships. It does not appeal to either identifications or sentiments. Identification with my family does not, as on the communal model, explain my communal obligations. Rather, it reflects the degree to which in undertaking these obligations I make the securing of my family's well-being through their fulfilment crucial to my ethical goals. I could distance myself from this end, performing my role as a mere formalism, in which case I would not have made this identification. In this instance people typically do not, though they vary greatly in their degree of identification or alienation with respect to other roles. Similarly we do not need to appeal to sentiments as the driving force behind the performance of obligations. Again the sentiments involved can be explained in terms of the demands of the role rather than vice versa. For in my parental role, for example, as in many other roles but certainly not all, I am related to particular people to whom I develop strong feelings of love and concern because of what my role entitles them to expect from me if I am performing it wholeheartedly. Making their particular well-being a crucial ethical goal *is* to love and have concern for them. This alternative interpretation of the ethics of special obligations within the family unsettles the sort of identity politics, like David Miller's, which purports to ground national, rather than merely civic, obligations in realist claims about the scope of our concerns.

Cultural pretensions

There is a quite different view of the place of identities, especially national identities, in politics from the communal one. It takes a much more sympathetic view of the politics of identity than I have entertained, not because it espouses a view of it as simply inevitable, but because it sees it as morally desirable. I shall term this conception 'culturalism' and it consists of three separate claims. First it holds that there really are certain sorts of fairly clearly limited cultural groups, and people are correctly recognising their membership of these in identifying themselves as they do. Second, the existence of these groups supposedly consists in certain sorts of fact about their members, but is independent of facts about the members of other groups, so that the group would exist as it does, other things being equal, whatever other groups were like. And third, it is claimed that there are facts about this kind of cultural group which are relevant to the political organisation of its members, so that for example, in choosing secession, whether justified or not, they are basing their choice on cultural facts of a sort which might support such a claim. These culturalist claims may seem to be obviously true, for surely there *are* such cultural groups and the question that arises is how to accommodate them politically. But as we shall see, they are open to challenge.

Just as the communal account draws upon both the dysfunctionality of a political organisation that does not reflect people's identity and the values that can be realised by one that does, so does the cultural one. Here a state will be dysfunctional if it does not enable people to participate by utilising their own cultural resources and, if it does, then it will realise values of freedom and equality. That people should have political control over their own culture is not, then, just a matter of legitimacy, but also of justice. For, supposing a state to contain two such cultures, it will be treating the members of one unfairly if it conducts its business in, and uses its power to advance, only the other. This is just what assimilating states set out to do, aiming to build a national culture out of the dominant one by suppressing, more or less brutally, expression of the other, in the expectation that it will eventually disappear and its members reacculturate. This is, for example, the principal reason for the Kurdish insurgency in Turkey. The situation is somewhat different where a state merely excludes a certain cultural group from political participation by discrimination against their culture, without any expectation or hope of their eventual assimilation – as is the case with many indigenous peoples in South American states, India and elsewhere. Both kinds of situation have fostered wars, either for separate government or for recognition and cultural rights. To the extent that these are defensive campaigns against injustice they need to be assessed along the lines suggested in Chapter 2. Whether there is any principled way of viewing them as responses to the denial of legitimate government is what concerns us now.

Why should people have a right to self-government through possession of their own culture? A variety of arguments could be made. One influential rationale advanced by Will Kymlicka, which we may term 'cultural contextualism', turns upon the idea that individuals typically participate in their own 'societal culture', that is to say 'a territorially concentrated culture, centred on a shared language which is used in a wide range of societal institutions, in both public and private life'.[30] Such a culture provides 'the media through which we come to an awareness of the options available to us' and is, therefore, 'a precondition of making intelligent judgements about how to lead our lives'.[31] That is to say, the sharing of a societal culture equips us with the necessary context for our choosing how to act freely: 'Freedom involves making choices amongst various options and one's societal culture not only provides these options, but also makes them meaningful to one.'[32] Self-government protects such cultures and may thus be necessary for safeguarding individual freedom itself. The cultural contextualist argument is thus a liberal one, of a sort that the makers of the Versailles settlement of 1919 could have embraced. Like them, its proponents too are sympathetic to the aspirations of 'small nations', equating those who are to exercise a right of self-determination with those who speak a distinct language within a territory.

Unlike the communal account – for which a shared culture comprises a range of common characteristics including values, since it is up to members to determine what its scope shall be – the cultural contextualist account deliberately excludes values from what counts as a societal culture. Values cannot be part of it since values are what are chosen within it, so that the same culture can, on this understanding, change its character, but not its essential nature as its members' way of life alters to realise different values. Were things otherwise, it would not have the merit that it does in making freedom possible, for the inclusion of values within the culture would restrict freedom, not facilitate it. What those who lose their societal culture, like many members of indigenous groups, are liable to, on this account, is anomie – an incapacity to make any meaningful choices about their lives, as the context for making choices disappears. It can, therefore, be maintained that one has not only a right but a duty to preserve one's culture, and hence to seek self-government if this is needed for it, which derives from one's duty as an individual to live one's life in a responsible and rational way.

Yet why, we may ask, does it matter if people lose their original culture so long as they acquire another within which they may make their choices? For this is what assimilation aims to do. Sometimes it fails and it is then, it may be suggested, that rootlessness and anomie result, but often indigenous peoples become absorbed into mainstream culture quite easily. John Stuart Mill held something like this view, arguing that French culture, for example, provided a better context for choices than Breton or Basque culture.[33] Cultural contextualists, however, view such a change, while possible as demonstrated by the acculturation of immigrants, as never generally desirable and always perilous. They do so because they embrace a functionalist conception of culture, whereby society is a system that maintains its own stability as a result of individual behaviour being regulated to maintain this end through conforming to the practices that the culture makes possible and meaningful.[34] On this account it is clear why assimilation is such a threat, since externally imposed change threatens the functional integrity of the culture within which choices are meaningful. Self-government, by contrast, ensures that changes which are made to the culture arise from within it and ensure its continuing effectiveness in enabling its members to act in changing circumstances.

Unfortunately the functionalist conception of 'a world of separate peoples, each with their own culture and each organised in a society which can legitimately be isolated for description as an island in itself' lacks any empirical plausibility.[35] It merely reflects the romanticism of thinkers like Herder and their anthropological followers which has so greatly influenced nationalism, especially ethnic nationalism, and continues to influence it. There is little reason to think that there are separate cultural groups differentiated in the way functionalism supposes. Rather it is the case that people share some of their cultural characteristics – language, say – with some others, other characteristics – various practices and institutions – with a different group, and so on. The components of culture sort us out in overlapping ways, not in neatly segregated groups. This is not to deny that people do often think of themselves as forming such groups, but the way they do gives no special prominence to language, so that members can identify themselves by race, religion, values and other characteristics excluded from the contextualist account as irrelevant to the availability of options for choice.

Cultural contextualism seeks to show how a collective identity which is relevant to this organisation is secured by membership of a societal culture. Yet, given the way people do actually identify themselves, this contextualist identity is one which may be quite obscure to them, so that the identity they profess and the one they actually possess on this account may come apart. The Serbs, Croats and Bosnian Muslims would simply have been wrong to suppose they had distinct national identities if their reason for thinking they had was that they differed in religion, for they all spoke Serbo-Croat and shared institutions in the land of the Southern Slavs. Perhaps they *were* wrong, but the categorisation of national groups is not so simple as cultural contextualism supposes.

Cultural contextualism is, however, not only empirically implausible in failing to recognise the multiplicity of ways in which people do actually group themselves, in the hope of discovering a stable and consistent pattern of groupings which would enable political claims to be adjudicated. Its method of finding such a pattern, by excluding religious and other values as possible differentiating features between national or other politically relevant groups, is itself tied to a particular value system, namely liberalism. For it is because autonomy, the freedom to choose one's own values, is valorised that values are excluded from a culture. Yet such liberal values are rejected in many cultures as destructive of community, endangering of religious belief or whatever.[36] Thus this principle of counting cultures will itself be rejected by many of them. Nor is Kymlicka right to argue that if cultures are distinguished from each other in terms of features other than values, then they do not necessarily share common values. Arguably, these are needed, at least for cultural communities with their common purposes.[37] Indeed, liberal societies may be thought of as sharing such public values, whatever room they leave for private choice and however differentiated they are in terms of language and history. What makes them communities would be, in part, the values their members share; what makes them culturally distinct, their languages and histories.

The myth of legitimacy

The politics of identity advances its political claims for separate statehood or special recognition in the belief that the state should be, somehow, a people's own. That is how their culture is held to be relevant to politics. For it is because a state corresponds appropriately in its boundaries or organisation to their culture that it is held to be their own state; and that is because they are taken to be identified primarily as members of the culture or as members of a community with a particular culture, so that the state corresponds to its citizens' identities. If and only if it does so correspond is the state supposedly legitimate. Thus a major cause of new wars is, as we noticed at the outset, the alleged failure of an existing state to recognise appropriately the putatively distinct identity of some section of its population and thereby to show itself as not their own – not their legitimate state.

The communal account, however, does not provide any adequate criterion of legitimacy. 'Nations exist,' writes Miller, 'when their members recognise one another as compatriots, and believe they share characteristics of the relevant kind.'[38] This would be fine if there were just one set of characteristics which distinguish nations (or whatever groups we are meant to feel loyalty to) from each other – a distinctive language, say. But as we have seen there is not. Some groups define themselves in terms of language, some by religion, yet others by other features of their way of life, history, or whatever. And these different grounds of nationality compete for members' allegiance, so that there is no stable and consistent answer to the question: with what group do they identify? This fact destroys the plausibility of any naturalistic account of group identification, but it also undermines theories, like Miller's, which purport to pick out the groups with certain political claims in terms of facts about people's loyalties. The competing criteria that people employ in determining where their loyalties lie implies that there can be no definitive way of dividing them up into nations, and therefore no way of deciding which political claims are justified and which are not. This kind of politics of identity is as useless in resolving political disputes rationally as it is fecund in producing the wars that seek to settle them by force.

Nor does culturalism supply a criterion of legitimacy. Anti-culturalists deny all three of the culturalist's propositions. Firstly, they deny that self-identification as a member of a national group constituted in terms of the sorts of cultural features we have mentioned is a matter of recognising some fact that other people could in principle also recognise about them and that they themselves could be ignorant of. Instead it is a matter of people deciding how to identify themselves and creating a group by their collective decision. Second, anti-culturalists hold that the resulting existence of the national group depends, not just upon the presence of features that its members select as constitutive of group identity, but upon the fact that these factors are selected as differentiating them from members of specific groups of others. Third, anti-culturalists view cultural groups so constituted as so far having no claim to separate statehood, or indeed, any special political arrangement. If any such groups do have a justifiable claim then it is due to other factors than that they are cultural groups of the kind they are. So the question that arises is, rather, how the fact that groups do so differentiate themselves is relevant to politics.

What I have termed 'the politics of identity' is often referred to as 'the politics of difference'.[39] We might, if we liked, appropriate these two terms for the same phenomenon (so far as its nationalist and analogous manifestations are concerned) viewed now through culturalist eyes, now through anti-culturalist ones. The actual participants in such political programmes are likely to think of themselves as claiming a firmly grounded and politically significant identity rather than merely marking a difference from others in the course of a campaign to have this difference recognised politically. This is because they will characteristically hold that it is not just because they are different that they warrant separate government, but because what makes them different is some feature that would justify their having their own government. It may, for example, be because Azerbaijanis are Muslims and Armenians Christians that they want states corresponding to the religions of their populations (so long as territory is not thereby lost) but this is because they think that their religion is an important part of their identity and for that reason should be reflected in their political arrangements, not just because they have come to differentiate themselves from the other along religious lines in a drive for political separation.

Anti-culturalists do not, of course, deny the importance to peoples' identities of features like religion. Rather they distinguish the mere possession of such cultural features from membership of groups defined in terms of them, on the grounds that participation in a culture is not necessarily tied intimately to membership of such a group, so that these groups may be far more ephemeral and superficial than are the cultural features which shape them. We can see this clearly in the Armenian/Azerbaijani war. For though there has been a protracted history of clashes, these have been neither continuous nor constant in their character. Azerbaijani national identity is a recent growth, following a period in the early twentieth century when Azeris identified themselves with other Turkic-speaking peoples of the region and conflict was largely based on language differences, partly resulting from resentment at the immigration of relatively well-educated Armenians in the wake of the Turkish genocide. Yet the deliberate construction under Soviet rule of a specifically Azerbaijani identity was in part due to anxieties that differentiation along religious lines would lead Muslim citizens across the republics to unite, creating a dangerous power bloc. Religious differences are now probably the larger cause of tension, following the revival of Islamic political identification worldwide.

We can see from this and many other examples how fluid group identifications are and this provides evidence which favours anti-culturalism. Indeed, it has often puzzled theorists why national identities – those most commonly cited as providing reasons for particular political arrangements – should be so various. Some seem to be founded on language, others on religion; some on historical and others on geographical factors; the diversity proliferates. Since J.S. Mill it has been customary to bring order to this lack of uniformity in the 'objective' features of national identity by alluding to 'subjective' ones – the common sympathies of those who share it, which may arise from various 'causes' as Mill calls them.[40] But causes are not necessarily reasons, and the issue between culturalists and anti-culturalists is, in part, whether the factors whereby people identify themselves collectively provide good reasons for their differentiation. The culturalist believes, that, in at least very many cases, they do, and develops a politics accordingly. Then, however, he owes us an account of why they are so diverse, and, since so diverse, how they can severally justify political divisions. The anti-culturalist, by contrast, explains the diversity of national identities in terms of the variety of ways in which people may differentiate themselves from one another and sees political division as just one aspect of that, not susceptible to a general explanation. Rather it is the case that group differentiation occurs for various reasons and serves varied interests – some good, some bad. In other words the underlying reasons for political divisions, actual or desired, lie elsewhere than in the prior existence of distinct cultural groups.

It is a fact from which we cannot escape that no principle of national self-determination or any other systemic principle of political organisation is workable, since nationalists disagree on what nations there are.[41] Each can generalise his own criterion to categorise the peoples of the world into separate nations, but his own criterion will be disputed by others. This is, indeed, the source of many conflicts, some of them violent, and the reason for violence is, in part, that no rational choice can be made between the rival criteria. Yet if a principle of national self-determination is to be allowed then some choice must be made in order for states to form a system, so that if the right is to be allowed a systematic identification of nations is required. No doubt for particular reasons and in particular circumstances pragmatic choices can be made about which groups should be allowed separate statehood. We have noted some in Chapter 2. But this is a very different matter from allowing a systemic right whose denial deprives the state of legitimacy.

Why does this proliferation of different criteria exist? Why is there this particular source of conflict? It depends, as I have said, on the notion that to be legitimate a state must be a people's own, in the strong sense of corresponding suitably to their identities, be these chosen or given. Without this notion, which cannot be sustained, there would be no such conflicts. Its source is a politics of identity that develops from attempts to gain voluntary support for established states, perhaps especially in war itself. Once generated to legitimise established states, the various criteria of national identity can be borrowed by dissatisfied groups to challenge their current civic membership.

Two kinds of answer can be given as to why the particular criteria of identity that are so employed are chosen. Doubtless they interact. One is a purely instrumental conception whereby a group appropriates the criterion that best fits its circumstances and maximises its support – a linguistic one if there is a widely shared language, a religious one if religion is already a strong tie, and so forth. The other kind of answer will point to cultural differences between groups that seek to legitimise their causes in different ways. The criteria of various sorts of voluntary association, typical of many civic nationalisms, arise from liberal traditions of thought about political organisation which may have little resonance with those groups which have not lived in liberal states or encountered the particular historical circumstances to which they are a response. Some ethnic criteria, by contrast, may seem natural in societies with close kinship ties over large areas, and quite alien to those without them (though even in such societies these ties might be romantically supposed to exist when they have no natural foothold). Whether language or religion counts may again depend upon whether the one or the other provides a social cement at the requisite level of organisation. The list could be extended indefinitely. What this shows is that it will appear culturally discriminatory to prefer one sort of criterion to another, given that none, if I am right, has any compelling transcultural rationale. Odious as many versions of ethnic or religious nationalism will seem to liberals, the way to curb their influence is not to embrace another nationalism – 'civic' being the liberals' preferred choice – but to reject nationalism itself as a basis for the legitimacy of states and with it any analogous forms of the politics of identity.

It is for this reason that it is in my view quite misguided indiscriminately to place the blame for new wars upon ethnic nationalism and similar manifestations of identity politics, either, as on the dark gods' theory as natural phenomena to be held in check, or on others, as embodying morally reprehensible principles of political organisation. People who suffer at the hands of 'nationalising states' may be forced to adopt an alternative politics to that with which a formal and quiescent citizenship provides them.[42] Yet this is a matter for regret and readjustment, not a reason for accepting the politics of identity as a desirable modality for ordinary political life nor even as a general feature which must simply be accepted and adapted to.

Notes

1. Russell F. Farnen, Introduction, in R.F. Farnen (ed.), *Nationalism, Ethnicity and Identity* (New Brunswick: Transaction, 1994), p. 3.
2. Zygmunt Bauman, *Postmodern Ethics* (Oxford: Blackwell, 1993), p. 230.
3. Ernest Gellner quoted David McCrone, *The Sociology of Nationalism* (London: Routledge, 1998), p. 8. The 'dark gods' theory is also known as 'primordialism'.
4. Quoted Nicholas Mansergh, *The Coming of the First World War* (London: Longmans, 1949), p. 245.
5. Michael Ignatieff, *Blood and Belonging* (London: Vintage, 1994), p. 14.
6. Quoted in *The Warrior's Honour* (London: Vintage, 1999), p. 61.
7. William Pfaff, *The Wrath of Nations*: Civilisation and the Furies of Nationalism (New York: Simon & Schuster, 1993), p. 57.
8. Sigmund Freud, *Group Psychology and the Analysis of the Ego* (1921). *Complete Psychological Works*, vol. XVIII (London: Hogarth Press, 1955), p. 113.
9. Ibid., p. 116.
10. Following Peter Gay, *Freud* (London: Macmillan, 1988), p. 406.
11. Sigmund Freud, *Group Psychology*, p. 100.
12. Ibid., p. 103.

13. Sigmund Freud, *Civilisation and its Discontents* (1930). *Complete Psychological Works*, vol. XXI (London: Hogarth Press, 1961), p. 109.

14. Michael Ignatieff, *The Warrior's Honour*, p. 57.

15. Sigmund Freud, *Group Psychology*, p. 97.

16. Ibid., p. 101.

17. Michael Ignatieff, *The Warrior's Honour*, pp. 50–1. He seems to half-recognise this in accusing Freud of muddying the distinction between major and minor differences.

18. Sigmund Freud, *Group Psychology*, p. 102.

19. Cp. 'It is scientifically incorrect that war or any other violent behaviour is genetically programmed into our human nature', *Seville Statement on Violence*, quoted David G. Myers, *Social Psychology* (New York: McGraw-Hill, 1993), p. 425.

20. *Pace* Michael Ignatieff, *The Warrior's Honour*, p. 45; William Pfaff, *The Wrath of Nations*, pp. 237–8.

21. Clifford Geertz, *The Interpretation of Cultures* (London: Fontana, 1973), p. 259.

22. Walker Connor, *Ethno-nationalism* (Princeton: Princeton University Press, 1994), pp. 203–4. The Freud citation is from *Complete Psychological Works*, vol. XX (London: Hogarth Press, 1925–6), pp. 273–4.

23. For criticism see Bernard Yack, 'The Myth of the Civic Nation', in R. Beiner (ed.), *Theorising Nationalism* (Albany: State University of New York Press, 1999); and Will Kymlicka, *Politics in the Vernacular* (Oxford: Oxford University Press, 2001), ch. 12.

24. Walker Connor, *Ethno-nationalism*, p. 206.

25. Quoted Frank Pakenham, *Born to Believe* (London: Cape, 1953), p. 72.

26. David Miller, *On Nationality* (Oxford: Clarendon Press, 1995), p. 121.

27. Ross Poole, *Morality and Modernity* (London: Routledge, 1991), p. 101.

28. F.M. Barnard (ed.), *J.G. Herder on Social and Political Culture* (Cambridge: Cambridge University Press, 1969), p. 324.

29. Quoted David Miller, *On Nationality*, p. 58.

30. Will Kymlicka, *Politics in the Vernacular*, p. 25.

31. Will Kymlicka, *Liberalism, Community and Culture* (Oxford: Oxford University Press, 1989), pp. 165–6.

32. Will Kymlicka, *Politics in the Vernacular*, p. 209.

33. Cp. John Stuart Mill, *On Liberty, Representative Government, the Subjection of Women* (London: Oxford University Press, 1912), p. 385.

34. See my *Peoples, Cultures and Nations in Political Philosophy* (Edinburgh: Edinburgh University Press, 2000), pp. 35–8.

35. Fredrik Barth, quoted ibid., p. 211.

36. See Bhikhu Parekh, *Rethinking Multiculturalism* (Houndmills: Macmillan, 2000), chs 3 and 11.

37. See Andrew Mason, *Community, Solidarity and Belonging* (Cambridge: Cambridge University Press, 2000), pp. 20–7.

38. Andrew Mason, *Community*, p. 22.
39. Iris Marion Young's distinction between these notions does not quite coincide with mine: see her 'Difference as a Resource for Democratic Communication', in J. Rohman & W. Rehg (eds), *Deliberative Democracy* (Cambridge, MA: MIT Press, 1997).
40. John Stuart Mill, On *Liberty*, p. 380.
41. This has been apparent at least since E.H. Carr, *Conditions of Peace* (London: Macmillan, 1942), ch. 3. It is the theme of my *The Philosophy of Nationalism* (Boulder: Westview, 1998), subsequently elaborated by Jacob T. Levy, *The Multiculturalism of Fear* (Oxford: Oxford University Press, 2000), ch. 3.
42. Cp. Rogers Brubaker, *Nationalism Reframed* (Cambridge: Cambridge University Press, 1996), ch. 1.

4

Hatred and Revenge

Recognition

There are, writes Thomas Hobbes, 'three principal causes of quarell. First, Competition; Secondly, Diffidence; Thirdly, Glory'.[1] Violence is used, he says, in the first and second cases, to acquire the goods of others or to defend one's own; in the third, 'for trifles, as a word, a smile, a different opinion, or any other signe of undervalue, either direct in their Person, or by reflection in their Kindred, their Friends, their Nation, their Profession, or their Name'. A 'signe of undervalue . . . in their Nation' is an even more potent cause for people to go to war than it was in Hobbes's day, not least because of the pernicious doctrine of national self-determination which we have just been examining. For to deny statehood to one putative nation when others have it may seem to undervalue it and hence to depreciate its glory. Conversely, the demand for a separate state reflecting a distinct collective identity, usually a national one, is a demand for a certain sort of recognition – recognition that is likely to have been withheld in a variety of other ways which supposedly undervalue the group, whether it is by cultural discrimination, religious intolerance or whatever, serious, trifling or even imaginary, since the measure of undervalue is its own sense of what is due. All such depreciation is understandably resented. Political independence is intended both to remove the victims from its influence and award them the recognition that depreciation denies.

Arguably the majority of new wars are caused by 'Glory'. Sikh terrorism in support of a 'Khalistan' state independent of India is just one example among others which illustrates the process. It was surprising to Indians that a violent separatist campaign should have emerged in the 1980s among the Sikhs, who have been singularly successful economically and politically, not only in Punjab, where they are concentrated, but across India as a whole. Despite these facts their charismatic leader, Sant Jarnal Singh Bhindranwali, complained that: 'Sikhs are living like slaves in independent India. Today every Sikh considers himself a second rate citizen...How can Sikhs tolerate this?'[2] The movement for Khalistan was intended to restore Sikh dignity. But what led its followers to suppose that they were in danger of losing it?

A number of factors seem to be involved. First, the history of the Sikhs is one of military defence of their religion – a blend of Hindu and Muslim elements – culminating in the establishment of the Sikh kingdom of Maharajah Ranjit Singh which had to confront both a Muslim *jihad* against them and the British advances into India. 'The Khalsa [= the pure, i.e. Sikhs] shall rule,' their last guru, Gobind Singh, had proclaimed.[3] Even in British India the Sikhs enjoyed a special position, forming one of the so-called 'martial races' from which the colonial power recruited to control its empire. In a predominantly Hindu India, following partition and independence, the Sikhs no longer enjoyed their previous status.

Their leaders, like Bhindranwali, also believed that their religion was in danger of losing its distinctiveness and being reabsorbed into the Hinduism from which it had sprung. There had always been a variety of practice within Sikhism, much of it almost indistinguishable from Hinduism, whose caste structure it shares. The language – Punjabi – is common to Sikhs, Hindus and Muslims. Relations between members of the religious groups are generally good, with communal violence erupting mainly in response to terrorist or counter-terrorist incidents. If the point of Sikh distinctiveness, religion, was under threat then there was a danger to Sikh self-esteem. Bhindranwali claimed that the scriptures revered by all Sikhs were insulted by Hindus and thus aimed to foster a collective pride in Sikh identity which would overcome internal differences and accentuate external ones. The image of a separate Sikh state offers a focus for Sikh aspirations, and the rise of Hindu nationalism provides a political context in which it seems to be required if they are to be attained. Any apparent progress towards a Sikh state then becomes a source of national pride, any setback an occasion of shame, to be resisted by violence if necessary.

This kind of pattern can be discerned in very many cases where groups are constructed as national, in the sense of having the kind of aspirations of which a desire for separate statehood is paradigmatic, and go on to wage violent campaigns against established states. A special respect which people take, for historical or other reasons, to be their due, is not accorded them. This is read both as discrimination and as a denial of the point of distinction in virtue of which respect is claimed. If the point of distinction is one that collects people together into a group then this may be construed as tantamount to a denial of due recognition to the group. The remedy must, therefore, be a collective one. Individual pride in the distinguishing characteristic – religion, language or whatever – can be reclaimed only by identifying with the group and ensuring its separate existence. The ideology of nationalism here provides a most dangerous mode of achieving this. And now progress to statehood or the lack of it can itself be interpreted as a succession of acknowledgements or slights, quite independent of those that originally set the movement in train.

How are we to assess this kind of situation ethically? One of the tendencies of recent thought about the politics of identity is to perceive it as a 'politics of recognition' and, as such, to adopt a sympathetic view of its claims – a view quite independent of any characterisation of the identity groups involved as communities or cultures of the kinds we looked at in the last chapter.[4] Rather the argument is that national groups have a right to statehood because they provide 'an anchor . . . for self-identification and secure belonging . . . People's . . . self-respect is affected by the esteem in which these groups are held.'[5] Unless national groups have parity with each other in terms of the political arrangements they enjoy they will not be being treated with equal esteem, and consequently nor will their members. But since the members' self esteem is intimately bound up with their national identity, denying recognition to their nation deprives them as individuals of that to which they have as much right as security and well-being, namely their self-respect.[6] Without this, it might be suggested, their resort to violence is understandable, even if not condonable.

There are many problems with this sort of argument, which, like those of the last chapter, invites us to regard a frustrated national identity, if not as a just cause for war, then at least as one that must be accommodated if peace is to be secured. It presents people's identification with their nation either as, in the realist fashion, simply given or, in the liberal one, as a perfectly legitimate choice, in either case offering a proper source of self-respect. Yet there is a great deal that is wrong with the idea that it is national membership which is the source of self-respect, and the errors in the argument mirror the political moves made in, for example, the transition from a Sikh religious identity to a supposed Sikh national one. For, I shall argue, the argument starts off from acceptable premises about sources of self-esteem which pose no threat to anyone and derives a conclusion that lays the world open to the constant danger of war.

There is, of course, no difficulty at all in the idea that people may be proud of their religion, their language or many other components of their culture, and there is a close connection between what people take pride in and how they identify themselves. Roles once again provide a model for this. To take pride in one's teaching, as a university lecturer, for example, is possible only if the occupancy of this role is important to one's sense of who one is and what matters to one: 'a word, a smile ... or any other signe of undervalue' can upset one's self-esteem and be a cause of quarrel. If the undervaluation is not of one's individual performance but of the role of university teaching within a given society, say, then this may, if sufficiently general, elicit a collective response, perhaps even a boost in recruitment to one's professional association. But it is still one's teaching one takes pride in, not membership of any group of teachers. Indeed, one may have pride in the former but none in the latter, perhaps because of one's reservations about the group itself – as self-satisfied, disunited, or whatever – or about its other members.

What goes for this case can go for any cultural characteristic and for the collectivity of those who possess it; so much so that someone can identify herself in terms of the characteristic without at all thinking of herself as a member of a group in the strict sense of a collection of people who classify themselves as belonging together in virtue of this shared characteristic. She may have no clear conception of the nature or limits of such a collectivity, and nor need others. It is commonly categorisation by others that creates such a conception, and a sense of being depreciated as a member of a group can stem from this. In many cases such a sense is fully justified, as when a particular culturally characterised section of the population is routinely humiliated – for example, the

Roma and other travelling people, whose way of life leaves them ill-equipped to organise and resist. But often no real depreciation is involved, as when a former superior status is eroded; or when a political movement is seeking to build support by delineating a group in terms of certain cultural characteristics supposedly under threat yet a source of individual pride. Established states are just as likely as any anti-state movement to adopt this tactic as part of their nation building programmes. Here the aim is not, of course, political recognition not conceded, but the identification of members with the state itself, so that a slight to it becomes a slight to them, its quarrel theirs.

Pride and hatred

The politics of identity, I wish to claim, involves a reliance upon the tactics described in the preceding section (or similar ones), in that the construction of identity and difference is made in terms of characteristics that carry a specific type of emotional charge, namely in terms of people's perception of themselves and others as the sort of people they are – pride, shame, love and hatred being the paradigms here. Thus fear – Hobbes's 'diffidence' – may be a shared emotion that collects people together into a group, but not one constituted by a common identity. The same goes for indignation, anger, resentment or bitterness: all are feelings which can produce solidarity in the face of their objects, but, though they are directed against other people, they are directed against them for what they do – act unjustly towards us and so on – not for what they are. By contrast when we take pride in what people do or hate them for doing something, it is the people themselves we are proud of or hate: their acts reveal them as possible objects of such emotions, which may persist long after the acts that occasioned them are forgotten and can, indeed, exist without any such occasions.

That the politics of identity gives rise to violence stems, I want to argue, from these facts. They are what lead to new wars, in nearly all cases, breaching a fundamental principle of the just war within the tradition, though a principle obviously not codifiable in international law. I refer to the principle that for a war to be just it must be embarked upon with the right intention. The right intention is, in broad terms, the search for a just peace, but what are ruled out as permissible intentions are those that derive from such motives as hatred or contempt. Thus St Augustine censures: 'The eagerness to inflict harm, the cruelty in (disproportion-ate) revenge, the unsatisfied and insatiable spirit, the savagery in (indiscriminate) warring, the lust to dominate, and things like this.[7] For, as this passage illustrates, entering the war, and par-ticipating in it, with the wrong intentions in this sense affects the character of the war itself, so that it is not only the *jus ad bellum* requirements that are breached, but the *jus in bello* constraints as well. And this is exactly what we encounter in new wars.

The question that should concern us, then, is how an emo-tion like pride should turn from a perfectly proper emotional response to the valuable characteristics of ourselves and those to whom we are suitably related, into a force that leads to 'cruelty' and 'savagery'. In the previous section I identified the nationali-sation, so to speak, of such emotions as what creates the political conditions for new wars. But this does not yet tell us why such wars should have the character they so often do. For an explana-tion of this, one place to turn is Rousseau's account of the way in which *amour de soi* (self love) turns into *amour propre* (pride) which, all too easily, becomes inflamed and dangerous:

> *Amour de soi* is contented when our true needs are satisfied. But *amour propre*, which makes comparisons is never content and never could be, because this sentiment, preferring ourselves to others, also demands others to prefer us to themselves, which is impossible. This is how the gentle and affectionate passions are born of *amour de soi* and how the hateful and irascible passions are born of *amour propre*.[8]

Elsewhere Rousseau argues that when the passions guided by *amour de soi*:

> are turned away from their object by obstacles, they become more concerned with the object to avoid it than with the object, so as to obtain it. They then change their nature and become angry and hate filled. This is how *amour de soi*, which is a good and absolute feeling becomes *amour propre* which is a relative feeling by which we compare ourselves. *Amour propre* . . . seeks its satisfaction, not in our own well-being, but only in the ills of others.[9]

However, neither part of this account of how proper pride can turn to hatred is intelligible without our realising that one of a person's 'true needs' is a social need for the 'consideration' of others – the 'wish to be looked at himself', the 'need to attach his heart';[10] and this is, so far, an 'absolute', not a 'relative' feeling.

Self-esteem, on Rousseau's account, requires the 'considera-tion of others', for a person cannot take pride in things which others do not value at all and for which they do not esteem him. He is able to 'attach his heart' to those who do. There is here, then, an account of social relations and the formation of social bonds. But it is not an account of the formation of social groups, since so far there is no indication of where any boundary between those with whom we have these bonds and those we do not lies. Yet what Rousseau says about the transition from a normal self love here to inflamed pride does suggest an account, though not one that Rousseau himself provides. For suppose we encounter others who do not value what we take pride in, because they take pride in something else – a different religion, say. Then indeed it is asking the impossible of them to show us the same sort of esteem our fellows do. Here we encounter an obstacle in our drive for the consideration of others, but one that we will only experience as an obstacle if we compare their response to that of others. It is at this point, Rousseau maintains, that our proper pride in what we value turns to hatred of those who value something else. The origin of a certain sort of group can, one might maintain, be traced to the drawing of boundaries that are charged with emotions which have precisely this sort of history.

Is this avoidable? On the general point Rousseau himself seems undecided. He has been claimed to represent a transition from the idea of a hierarchical society within which there is a constant struggle for honour to a republican one in which people relate to one another in a 'politics of equal dignity' which resolves that restless search.[11] But even if this is so it tells us nothing about how republican societies relate to one another, and here Rousseau seems happy to draw upon the notion that a republic's members may be motivated by their *amour propre* in the group to give it their support, without fully embracing the conclusions he else-where derives about the dangers of this emotion. Perhaps this is because he views conflict with other groups as merely acciden-tal, if their internal unity derives from a common purpose rather than being constructed by their differentiating themselves from others. Yet if it is the latter that is involved – and arguably, as we have seen, in the politics of identity it must be (since a common purpose does not constitute a common character) – then is there inevitably a contest for honour between groups, which 'excites and multiplies the passions... making all men competitors, rivals, or rather enemies'?[12] Or can there be the equivalent of equal dignity between people at the level of inter-group relations?

It is by no means clear that we are entitled to any such comforting conclusion, for equal dignity is the consequence of a republican constitution for which there is no international equivalent. What there is, instead, is a convention that statesmen prescind from each others' identities in their international dealings, since clearly no effective dealings are possible between people who treat each other with the arrogance or contempt they may feel on account of their identities. But this is precisely to attempt to substitute, at the international level, a politics of role for a politics of identity. Where the latter rules instead, people may be plunged into the very conflicts of mutual hatred that Rousseau's account would lead one to predict. Since the ordinary members of different national groups, unlike statesmen, interact under no similar constraints of mutual respect, their behaviour towards one another in time of war or the threat of war may be expected to express the hatred born of wounded, or even merely vulnerable, pride that typifies new wars. Interacting, on the other hand, as citizens of political groupings with different interests they have the resources to show, instead, an understanding of each other's position, for they occupy the same roles vis-à-vis their different groups. They can, therefore, even admire each others' performance of their roles, conflicting as their objectives may be. This goes a long way towards enabling statesman and citizen alike to satisfy the requirement of right intention, the former in entering a war, the latter in participating in it or giving it their support.

Revenge

Conflicts of interest generate no necessary cycle of violence. If war is resorted to then its costs are a disbenefit to be weighed against the interest that it seeks to secure. Sooner or later the calculation will probably yield a desire for peace, even though interests remain unsecured. It is quite a different matter in the competition for honour involved in wars of national identity and pride. For here violence is resorted to in order to avenge a 'signe of undervalue' in Hobbes's phrase. Revenge is retaliation designed to subject another to a similar humiliation as that which he has imposed on one or, perhaps preferably, a worse shame. This will nearly inevitably elicit, in its turn, a violent response, and so a cycle of revenge is set in train. The problem is that although revenge is essentially 'paying someone back' for what he has done to one, there is no measure of what constitutes fair payment. 'Getting even' is seldom a description accepted by the person with whom one gets even. The reason depends upon a version of Rousseau's argument that '*amour propre* . . . can never be content' since it seeks the impossible. What makes a fair measure of payback impossible is the different estimation that each party has of what the injury or humiliation inflicted amounts to. For each party puts a higher estimate upon themselves, than those who injure them do. So what seems like getting even to the injured, seems disproportionate to the injurer, and so the cycle goes on.

It is important to distinguish here between revenge and retribution. The notion of retribution is that of inflicting suffering upon someone because they have deserved it, where the measure of desert is some impersonal system of punishment for wrong acts. Those who deliver retribution need feel no personal sense of outrage, even if they are, as usually they will not be, the party wronged. They may merely act to enforce compliance with a code of right and wrong, unlike the avenger, who must always act from a keen sense of personal injury. If both parties accept the code and acknowledge the system of enforcement then there can be closure, which is what a retributive account of punishment often stresses: to punish: 'is to annul the crime, which otherwise would have been held valid, and to restore the right' – that is to say, to return matters to an ethical status quo in which the wrong done is cancelled by retribution.[13] No such closure is possible, as we have seen, in the case of revenge.

In war it may be retribution rather than revenge that is claimed as the motive. In older understandings of just war this is, indeed, a feature of a right intention in waging it. For what is intended is the restoration of justice which due punishment for injustice brings so that, as Augustine says it is 'the wrong doing of the opposing party which compels the wise leader to wage just wars'.[14] This punitive version of the theory dominated medieval thinking, but, as we have seen, it has given way in modern times to the defensive version that we have been principally considering. The reason is perhaps not far to seek; for, while defence against aggression is usually a condition fairly easily established, the same cannot be said of the much more general condition of being wronged. This implies that while the responses appropriate to aggression can be codified internationally – as they have been, though not without difficulty, by the United Nations – nothing similar is possible with respect to 'wrong doing'.[15] This may comprise a wide variety of actions for the punishment of which their supposed victim may resort to war, including actions which can constitute injustices only on the assumptions of the victim, and not on any general principles which can be mutually accepted. It is evident that these cannot be subject to international codification, so that acts of war to rectify them cannot be justified as retribution whose imposition upholds the international order.

This sort of unilaterally perceived injustice has been an especially potent cause of war – in new wars it threatens to be so again. The medieval crusades, for example, were fought to recover the Holy Land from the Muslims since it was held to be, 'rightfully Christian property, for it had been consecrated by the presence of Christ and conquered by the Roman, later to be the Christian, Empire in a just war'.[16] Needless to say such reasoning would not have been convincing to the Muslims. Indeed preachers had some difficulty persuading Christians, one of them envisaging that: 'someone says, "The Muslims have not hurt me at all. Why should I take the Cross against them?" But if he thought well about it he would understand that the Muslims do great injury to every Christian.'[17]

Exactly the same considerations apply to wars fought for similar causes, as, for example, in those cases of *jihad* where the settlement of other peoples on supposedly Muslim land needs to be rectified and punished. In many such cases, as palpably in the crusading message, an identity is appealed to beyond that of membership of an existing political entity. For it is not a wrong to such an entity which calls for retribution, but one to a people characterised by a culture that carries with it distinctive standards of justice and injustice, as religious cultures commonly do. It is evident that retaliation for an injury so conceived cannot possess the deterrent effect of retaliation against aggression, which thereby becomes itself an act of self-defence and not just retribution.

It is equally evident that retribution for an injury of which the injured party is the sole judge does not differ sufficiently significantly from revenge to provide closure to prevent a cycle of violence. Where this situation prevails the sense that one's *own* code has been breached is likely to induce all those feelings of animosity which make revenge so dangerous. Nor, when war is being waged to visit retribution upon wrong doers, are there any of the safeguards of institutionalisation that can exist when this situation pertains in the setting of domestic law enforcement. The idea that 'the feeling of hatred and the desire of vengeance . . . are important elements of human nature which ought . . . to be satisfied in a regular and public manner' by punishing 'the grosser forms of vice' is a common defence of retributive punishment.[18] But the distinction it draws between private vengeance and public punishment cannot be carried over to the case of punitive war, for even when this is waged under proper authority the authority in question represents the supposedly wronged party, not a body that stands outside and above the relationship of criminal to victim.

It is a cardinal principle of the just war that, both in waging it at all and in the manner of waging it, proportionality must be observed; that is to say, retaliation must not be out of proportion in the human suffering it occasions to that of the wrong incurred or attack repulsed. This may be reasonably easy to gauge in a conventional defensive war, where what degree of force sufficient to protect a people and deter aggression is calculable. It will be apparent from the foregoing argument that no such calculation will be available in a punitive war where the aggrieved party is the judge of its own injury. What constitutes a proportionate response in the eyes of the injured party will probably seem disproportionate to the other, as in the case of revenge, and violence will escalate. It is a situation all too often observed in new wars, where sub-state groups construe their treatment as warranting an armed response, the dignity of the state is seriously affronted and a large scale repression of dissent is mounted, this fuels resentment and support for armed opposition, and so the spiral mounts.

Nowhere can this be seen more vividly than in the case of reprisals. 'Reprisal' is a technical concept in military law,[19] connoting acts that are in themselves contrary to the laws of war, for example attacks upon civilians, but that are taken as a response to lawless acts by the enemy. They are aimed at deterring such lawlessness and hence at enforcing the laws of war, and as such are permitted, with certain exceptions, so long as they are proportionate to the lawless act. At the best of times reprisals are a dangerous weapon, provoking counter-reprisals and escalating attacks normally illegitimate, as when, in World War II area bombing culminated in the indiscriminate German V-bomb, (where V stands for *Vergeltung* = reprisal). They are, perhaps, licensed as much because, as vengeful reactions to gross violations of the military code, they are inevitable, as for any genuine faith in their efficacy in enforcing it. Yet in new wars reprisals are taken, not in any expectation of regulating the conduct of armed conflict, but simply as tit-for-tat actions, perhaps sometimes deliberately designed to terrify whole sections of the population in the light of the lawlessness of some of their members, but mostly merely expressive of vengefulness and hate – emotions that find relief only when others are brought low because of what they are.

Nationalist sentiments

I have painted a very negative picture of the politics of identity in trying to account for its drive towards war, and this, objectors will say, is quite unfair; for the emotions on which the relevant sorts of identity are founded can be admirable ones, they will claim, not base or dangerous. Can they not be love rather than hatred, or humility rather than pride? Love of some shared object – country, faith or whatever; humility in the face of shared ideals or a shared history. We can, I think, quickly dismiss the latter suggestion. Feelings of humility about one's calling, say, are quite compatible with pride in it. Indeed, they seem to depend upon such a pride, for if one did not have it then the distance between the demands the calling made upon one and one's fulfilment of them would not be humbling. And if this is so any 'undervalue' of one's calling is again liable to have the sort of effects indicated earlier – effects that are potentially conflictual if one's calling is a collective one, and undervalue emanates from another group summoned by a different call. The perils of pride lie in wait for those who are personally humble as well as for those who are proud.

Love has its dangers too. In Rousseau's account of the development of social relations, he observes:

> A tender and sweet feeling insinuates itself into the soul, and at the least obstacle turned, becomes an impetuous fury; jealousy awakens with love; Discord triumphs, and the gentlest of passions receives sacrifices of human blood.[20]

So it is with the love of country, or of whatever else must be valued, if one is to lay claim to some national identity (or one of its analogues). For the politics of identity demands love, or something like it, from those it marshals in its service. Thus to be a good Englishman requires that one has a deep love of England, to be a good Muslim that one loves the Koran and so on. No similar feelings are required of the good citizen, say, or the good soldier. All that is required here is performance of the role: anything beyond risks being de trop – an emotional reaction that threatens to disrupt adherence to the constraints the role imposes, especially in the military case.

This is not, of course, to deny that *patriotism* may be required in either role. But patriotism is quite different in kind from the love of country required of nationalists.[21] It is, in the republican tradition carried down from Cicero, a form of dutifulness and esteem, expressed in acts of service and care towards fellow citizens and directed towards the political entity that makes citizenship a possible form of life. Much later Rousseau himself spells out the distinction between love of country as love for one's fellow citizens and love of the land. The former is a rational response, not susceptible, it would seem, to the kind of degeneration he speaks of in the passage just quoted. For it is not a species of love that needs to occupy the mind as 'a tender and sweet feeling' does, and hence it need not turn to 'impetuous fury'. The love of a land, by contrast, is construed, in most nationalist thinking, as a passional, rather than a rational, response – anterior to, not consequential upon, political organisation. Possession, in some sense, is its goal, as it cannot be the goal of a love of one's fellow citizens. It is acting to secure possession that love of a land motivates, not the regular performance of duties that manifests love of one's fellow citizens.

The grossest form of the desire for possession to which a nationalist love of country gives rise is, of course, a demand for exclusive occupation of its territory, and we need to ask why exclusivity is such a common concomitant of the kind of love of the land that is involved. It can have many other causes. It can simply reflect the interests, reasonable or predatory, of those who make the demand, whether, as often in the former case, indigenous inhabitants threatened with dispossession, or, in the latter, settlers who shape the land to their design. In either case the demand can lead to war, and to ways of pursuing the war that lead to the displacement of peoples. However, when linked to a politics of identity that motivates former neighbours to turn upon one another with violence the demand can lead to 'ethnic cleansing' or even genocide, acts not solely instrumental, but expressive of the resentment and jealousy that another's share in the possession of the land evokes – even when that share represents no serious threat to interests and would never be challenged were interests alone involved. The demand for exclusive occupation has deeper roots.

We can see this if we turn to other kinds of identity not founded upon a relation to land and when the sole possession demanded cannot stem from a material interest in its object. Consider, for example, religious identities associated with the veneration of sacred texts and the kind of exclusive possession of such texts that their adherents claim. In this case it is the appropriation of the text under one kind of interpretation rather than another, of the sort that divides Catholics and Protestants within Christianity, the former reading the scriptures through the traditions of the Church, the latter through the personal relationship of believers to God. Similar differences exist within Islam and other scriptural religions, and, as in the Christian case, can themselves provide a motivation for ethnic cleansing when employed to mark identities that are being mobilised politically. What is going on when the love even of a holy book can lead to sacrifices of human blood?

The key, I suggest, lies in the fact that the possession that the emotions of national and analogous identities seek is, at root, a shared perception of its object and of those other features of the world to which its object is salient. Just as a jealous lover fears that a rival has found in the beloved something that the lover cannot see, and therefore aims to deny its existence by removing the rival, so the nationalist lover of the country he claims as his alone resents the way an alien may think of and treat it, and just so is the religious lover of scripture moved by indignation at heretical readings of his text. Identities such as these are built upon a shared view of certain aspects of the world as revealed in common cultural representations and practices. In the love of country case these are characteristically to be found in particular ways of managing and depicting the landscape; in the religious one, in particular rituals. In either case the signs of another culture in the same public space are likely to appear an alien intrusion. The real threats, of course, commonly come from a quite different source – from the effects of economic change upon local customs. Their perpetrators are harder to discern than some foreign identity group; though pan-Islamists, for example, do so pick them out collectively as 'the West' and, as such, to be excluded from a unified Muslim world.

A shared perception of the world and what is of value within it, distinct from the perception had by others, can generate a certain sort of community. It is, one may say, community as communion.[22] The religious echo is appropriate, for what here brings people to identify themselves together is that they are 'united by a common agreement in the objects of their love...To observe the character of a particular people we must examine the objects of its love.'[23] This is St Augustine's definition of a people or community and it is devised specifically to individuate them in terms of shared values, especially religious ones. The criterion of membership is, one may say, confessional – a willingness to adopt the same credo as one's fellows. It is a quite different criterion from that of membership of a group with a common purpose in advancing collective interests, as is membership of a state or other political organisation. For whereas the expectations of the latter comprise the dutiful performance of a specific role, those of the former, as we saw in the previous chapter, are indeterminate. They depend, as we can now appreciate, upon members having the right emotions, so that their actions will be those that are required of them if and only if correctly motivated. But this, of course, unlike the performance of roles, can be assessed by no transcultural standards. How, then, can such emotions be acquired?

No doubt there are complex answers to this question. But one factor common in the politics of identity must be mentioned before we leave the subject of this chapter. It is the place of charismatic leaders in the campaigns of identity groups, especially those engaged in war. Max Weber, it may be recalled, distinguished three types of authority depending upon the motivations which lead to obedience: rational authority when a leader is obeyed because of his legal standing; traditional, when because of his customary position; and charismatic, when due solely to 'the extraordinary quality of the specific *person*',[24] the sort of quality that is exemplified politically, Weber suggests, in a successful warlord. But though success is needed for him to maintain his authority it is not its basis: that comes from recognition by his people. What is recognised, we may say, is that the charismatic leader instantiates and manifests in his person the character of the people he leads, and he does so because he is able to articulate, through word or action, 'the object of their love'. It is his example that they follow, but they do so not because they find in it something admirable on independent grounds. It is itself the measure of what is to be admired, and herein lies its ethical dangers. For, as Weber astutely observes, 'charisma knows only inner determination and inner restraint'.[25] But an inner restraint, unlike the restraints of rational or traditional office, is, as we see in the conduct of new wars by leaders like Slobadan Milosovicz or Osama Bin Laden, no adequate restraint at all.

Notes

1. Thomas Hobbes, *Leviathan* (many editions, 1651), ch. 13.
2. Quoted Paul Wallace, 'Political Violence and Terrorism in India: the Crisis of Identity', in M. Crenshaw (ed.), *Terrorism in Context* (University Park, PA: Pennsylvania State University Press, 1995), p. 360. The account that follows derives from Wallace's.
3. Quoted Donald L. Horowitz, *Ethnic Groups in Conflict* (Berkeley: University of California Press, 1985), pp. 204–5.
4. Cp. Charles Taylor, 'The Politics of Recognition', in A. Gutmann (ed.), *Multiculturalism* (Princeton: Princeton University Press, 1994).
5. A. Margalit & J. Raz, 'On National Self-Determination', in J. Raz *Ethics in the Public Domain* (Oxford: Clarendon Press, 1994), pp. 133–4.
6. Cp. John Rawls *The Law of Peoples* (Cambridge, MA: Harvard University Press, 1999), p. 34.
7. Quoted W.L. La Croix, *War and International Ethics* (Lanham: University Press of America, 1988), pp. 63–4.
8. Jean-Jacques Rousseau, *Emile* (1762), quoted Timothy O'Hagan, *Rousseau* (London: Routledge, 1999), p. 173. I am indebted to O'Hagan's discussion of *amour-propre*, ibid., ch. 4.
9. Jean-Jacques Rousseau, *Dialogues* (1772–6) quoted O'Hagan, *Rousseau*, p. 177.

10. Ibid. quoted Tzvetan Todorov, *Life in Common* (Lincoln, NB: University of Nebraska Press, 2001), pp. 12–13. Notice that Rousseau employs 'amour propre' sometimes for 'proper' and sometimes for 'improper' pride.
11. Charles Taylor, 'The Politics of Recognition', pp. 44–51.
12. Jean-Jacques Rousseau, *Discourses* (1750–55) quoted Tzvetan Todorov, *Life in Common*, p. 21.
13. G.W. Hegel, *Philosophy of Right* (trans. T.M. Knox, Oxford: Oxford University Press, 1942), p. 69.
14. Quoted La Croix, *War and International Ethics*, p. 63.
15. Cp. Geoffrey Best, *War and Law since 1945* (Oxford: Clarendon Press, 1994), pp. 182, 229.
16. Jonathan Riley-Smith, *What were the Crusades?* (Houndmills: Macmillan, 1977), p. 20.
17. Quoted ibid., p. 30.
18. James Fitzjames Stephen, quoted Ted Honderich, *Punishment: the Supposed Justifications* (Harmondsworth: Penguin, 1969), p. 29.
19. See Geoffrey Best, *War and Law since 1945*, pp. 311 ff.
20. Jean-Jacques Rousseau, *Discourses* (1750–55) quoted O'Hagan, *Rousseau*, p. 164.
21. For an extended treatment of this development see Maurizio Viroli, *For Love of Country* (Oxford: Oxford University Press, 1995).
22. Following Jean-Luc Nancy, discussed by Costas Douzinas, *The End of Human Rights* (Oxford: Hart, 2000), pp. 212 ff.
23. Augustine, *The City of God* (many editions) XIX 24.
24. H.H. Gerth & C. Wright Mills (eds.), *From Max Weber* (London: Routledge & Kegan Paul, 1970), p. 295.
25. Ibid., p. 246.

5

The Conduct of War

Extremism

The sorts of emotion that make it possible to mobilise people for new wars are characteristic of extremism. For they depend upon a valorised perception of one's own group and its world that is distinguished from the perception that other groups have in such a way that no common ground for the resolution of conflict may be found. 'Extremism' is, indeed, a vague term, connoting either the holding of extreme opinions or the advocacy of extreme courses of action, and there is a connection here, since opinions may perhaps be adjudged extreme when they issue in courses of action that are. This, I suggest, is a better way of conceiving of opinions as extreme than seeing them as diverging most widely from some political centre, thought of as the position with maximum political support; for there is no reason to think that a majority cannot hold extreme views – in many of our examples they surely do – so that extremism cannot be contrasted with centrism. Nor can it be contrasted with acceptance of the status quo, as radicalism is, since reactionary positions can be as extreme as radical ones.

Extremism actually contrasts with moderation. Such a mode of politics used to be known as 'trimming', from the analogy with the way one trims a boat to prevent too much weight on one side capsizing it.[1] For moderates distrust a politics in which the single minded pursuit of political objectives threatens to upset the stability of the system by engendering conflict that cannot be contained by normal politics. Extreme positions, then, are those that lead to courses of action outside the norms of ordinary politics life and even, as the trimmers saw in events like the English Civil War, to violence. The extremist, motivated by passionate belief

in and zeal for his cause, is unwilling to engage in ordinary political processes that lead to conciliation and compromise. Indeed,
he may despise such processes as themselves unprincipled, not
justified by commitment to any moral values but by the ignoble
desire for a quiet life. The moderate, therefore, has a contrasting
mistrust of theoretical positions, especially those moral ones that
are argued for on *a priori* grounds, rather than from experience.
She has a natural preference, therefore, for a politics conducted
in accordance with the restraints imposed by the occupation of
established roles.

We should not think that extremism is in some way a patholog-
ical psychological state, unable to accommodate the contradic-
tory impulses for, say, individual liberty and social order, which a
moderate politics must negotiate.[2] Far from being irrational, extremists may rationally calculate that their political ends require
the disruption of normal politics, within whose constraints they
are unlikely to be achieved. Nor should we necessarily think of
extremists as temperamentally intolerant of other views. In general, as I have indicated, they will pursue different ideals from
their opponents, but they may be quite tolerant of their different pursuits so long as they do not surface in the same public
and political sphere. It is within this that extremists are unwilling to admit opposition with all the demands for consultation
and mutual concession which it brings. Now such a moderate
politics is, one might think, what holds together people with different interests. Without it extremists cultivate an activist style
of politics in which a group is united around a common pursuit of its individuating values.[3] In such a politics to resort to
war provides opportunities for mobilisation of support which
are absent in normal politics. But just because of this it invites
the abuses common to new wars. For the conduct of war can
itself be moderate or extreme.

This may initially seem surprising. Looking at the awful facts
of war, we may feel compelled to agree, however reluctantly,
with the British admiral who wrote, 'The essence of war is violence. Moderation in war is imbecility. Hit first, hit hard, and
hit everywhere.'[4] What Admiral Fisher was expostulating about
was the Hague Convention of 1899 which sought to restrict the
means and methods of warfare. Its provisions reflect, and seek
to make more specific, some of the customary laws of war. For
the tradition of just war thinking has, of course, informed rules

not only about when war is permissible but also about what sort of actions are permissible in war – about what constitutes *jus in bello*. Resistance to such rules, 'militarism' as it is sometimes called,[5] is an aberration that commends the disturbance of settled norms for supposedly higher ends, not a sober description of those norms. Tolstoy, a pacifist, opposed the Hague Convention for the opposite reason from militarists. He believed that restraints in war disguised its real nature and thus made it easier to wage. The 'prohibition to use in strife all the means that exist' was he said 'impracticable' in the life and death struggle of war. Rather we should oppose war by viewing 'with contempt those who ... enter the ranks of those murderers, called soldiers'.[6]

This is not the place for a discussion of pacifism. But what, if we reject it, is the difference between murderers and soldiers? It is that soldiers perform a recognised role, broadly speaking that of engaging in a conflict of arms, which carries with it both certain permissions and certain constraints. This is a role which, non-pacifists can allow, makes possible one way of living a good life, by displaying virtues of courage, chivalry, loyalty and so on of a kind specific to the role. None of this can be said of murderers, whose acts fulfil no social function, carry no constraints and contribute nothing to a morally good life. But how can the same act – killing someone – have such a different character in the two cases? It is not, I suggest, because of a difference in the motive: a murderer's may be high minded – to rid the world of an evil man; a soldier's ignoble – to impress his comrades. Nor is it necessarily because of the consequences: they could be better in the former than in the latter case. That soldiers act under authority does not establish the required difference, for a government assassin may, for all that, be just a murderer; while that soldiers kill in personal self-defence, though often, is not always true.

Rather what makes the difference between the cases is precisely the scope and limits upon his targets and methods that a soldier's role creates and the purpose for which it creates them. Without such limits, Tolstoy would be right and soldiers be just murderers. But their targets and methods are limited by the principle of military necessity, that is to say, by what is needed to secure a victory over enemy troops. Such military engagements, furthermore, are not merely a deadly game, for which a space is found in social life. Upon their outcomes depends the fate of the ordinary people, whose defence is, as we have earlier seen, the only proper purpose of war. The role of soldiers is to fight on their behalf, so that were the distinction between those that fight or are fought, and those that are fought for to be eroded, so too would be the distinction between war and mass murder. Those who fight on behalf of others should command a certain sort of respect from those engaged in the same enterprise on the opposite side. So should those on whose behalf fighting is undertaken, if the protection of such people is to be valued as an aspect of a role shared on both sides. It is these sorts of respect that are reflected in the prohibitions of the rules of war.

What such prohibitions and permissions make possible are the military virtues without which the role of a soldier offers little and which are unavailable to mere murderers. Military courage, for example, is possible, in fact, because there are restraints in what one can do to an enemy and its people by way of protecting oneself. For courage requires the running of risks that could be avoided, and if risks could be avoided by unrestrained violence no courage would be displayed. Instead we would witness ruthlessness, callousness, or cruelty, which are vices because they fail to show humanity – which, together with necessity, is the guiding principle of the role. Chivalry requires respect for the forces and people of the enemy simply *qua* opponent in a conflict, and independent of their moral character. It is possible only if violence against them is constrained by the purpose of military conflict – the gaining of victory – and it is as codifying such constraints that the rules of war are recognised. It is, then, not just because the rules are broken that misconduct in war is dishonourable: it is because it fails to display the respect due to an opponent, and thus fails to show that one's performance of the role of soldier is in itself a source of self-respect, rather than merely a means to achieving other personal ends.

I have suggested that the norms of *jus in bello*, which we shall investigate in more detail shortly, derive from the role of a soldier. But it will be objected that this is itself determined by more general ethical considerations. It is this kind of argument that the moderate resists, replying that no general justification of the norms commands more plausibility than the regard we have for them to the extent that they explain what we take to be good or bad soldiery. These standards are developed over many years through reactions to particular military situations and developments. There is, the moderate argues, more reason to have faith in them than in any abstract values in terms of which they might be justified or reshaped. This is not to say that they are referable to no other considerations than those that directly concern soldiers in battle. While the purely customary law of war would appear to reflect mainly such concerns, codification in treaty law manifests the desire of statesmen to fulfil their duties to safeguard the lives of ordinary citizens and to maintain their security by minimising losses in war. But again it is because we require, as citizens, fulfilment of these duties by our statesmen, and not for some further reason, that we expect them, if they are performing their office well, to enter and honour treaties which regulate the conduct of war. If they do not then they fail us by exposing us all to greater perils.

How, though, can the international efforts of statesmen be carried over to control the internal conflicts that constitute so many new wars? Jurists recognise that since the parties to such conflicts are not under treaty obligations to each other they may have less motivation to comply with the rules of war but they are enjoined to implement them to the fullest degree possible.[7] Our discussion suggests that to the extent that the participants view themselves as acting in the role of soldiers they will do so. To the extent that their actions are conceived as having a different character they will not feel a need to. This, I have argued, is the underlying danger of extremism: it sets greater store upon the attainment of goals that realise values abstractly conceived than it does on the performance of established roles and thereby leaves us vulnerable to uncertainty in our moral relationships.

Proportionality

The Hague Convention and its successors gave rise to a body of international law about the means and methods of warfare conventionally labelled 'Hague Law'. Hague Law brings together the principles of necessity and humanity mentioned earlier in prohibiting certain ways of waging war as causing suffering beyond what is necessary to the achievement of strictly military objectives. On this basis the use of certain sorts of weapon is banned absolutely, from the notorious dum-dum bullet outlawed by the original 1899 Convention to chemical and biological weapons and, more recently, landmines. So is the use of certain tactics, such as indiscriminate bombardment. More broadly, it is impermissible to use any methods that are disproportionate in their effects to the military objectives that they achieve. This traditional *jus in bello* requirement of proportionality may be viewed as limiting what can legitimately be done in battle to that which is proper to a soldier's role: to cause suffering beyond what is strictly militarily needed is to step outside that role to occupy a different character, and can only proceed from motives that cannot be entertained within the role.

The rule of proportionality and its related prohibitions are often hard to discern in the way that the asymmetric and often internal conflicts of new wars are conducted. Extremists on either side are prone, as we have seen, to contemplate the use of *any* means to secure their overriding purposes. As the Russian anarchist Nechayev wrote of the revolutionary:

> Day and night he must have one single purpose: merciless destruction. To attain this goal, tirelessly and in a cold-blooded fashion, he must always be prepared to be destroyed and to destroy with his own hands everything that hinders its attainment.[8]

Of course not all participants in new wars adopt this attitude, but many do see their prospective long-term ends – universal freedom, for the anarchist – as justifying their short-term means however apparently costly in human suffering. It is important to see that the rule of proportionality does not license such a consequentialist calculation. It does not measure overall political ends, however morally commendable, against human suffering, but strictly military ones.[9] That is to say it presupposes that political leaders are confined in their lawful use of violence against armed opponents to military means. Their use of violence is construed as war or as intended war when directed against states or against groups with aspirations of statehood or to the control of states. Violent acts falling outside those permitted in war are therefore regarded as breaches of the rules of war or simply as crimes. Political leaders have no authority to order these nor soldiers to carry them out.

This implies that if we are to discern the rule of proportionality and its relations operating in new wars we must be able to regard them as properly wars, and not just outbreaks of uncontrolled violence between conflicting parties. They must, that is to say, be describable in terms of patterns of activity aimed at securing military objectives. Military objectives, in this context, comprise areas of land, supply lines, installations and so forth as well as enemy personnel and their equipment, whose capture, destruction or neutralisation contribute to a military victory, that is to say, to a situation in which the enemy is forced to capitulate in virtue of its comparative military weakness.[10] But new wars, as we noted at the outset, differ from the old precisely in lacking such a structure. If, on the one hand, a sub-state group has no expectation of obtaining military superiority over its opponent and, on the other, a state or combination of states has little hope of ending enemy operations by demonstrating its superior force then how can the operations of either be assessed as proportionate to purely military goals, or not as the case may be?

We can approach the problem by considering weapons and tactics that are in themselves prohibited. The thinking behind this ban is not just that these are too horrible to employ whatever the supposed military advantage, but that they do not properly constitute military means at all, since they cannot be employed in a way that forces the enemy to count their consequences only in the extent to which his forces are reduced in numbers or otherwise rendered incapable of action. The suffering and alarm they cause is ineluctably part of their purpose, not an unfortunate side effect. A warring party subjected to them must factor it into their considerations. Yet this is to be forced to view the progress of hostilities not principally as effecting changes in the balance of military advantage but as imposing relative degrees of suffering, so that the outcome is determined on the basis of which side is subjected to the more intolerable degree. It is tempting to suggest that no one could rationally assent to such a contest. Certainly to do so implies a valuation of ends in comparison with whose achievement the sufferings of unregulated war count measurably less and this is, perhaps, what we witness in new wars, especially those with religious ends. Such ends are unlikely, as we have seen, to be valued equally on either side, so that the contest becomes one in which the relative valuation of suffering, as well as its amount, decides the issue. What can safely be said, then, is that no one who does not identify herself with ends that value the avoidance of suffering comparatively little could rationally assent to a contest in which the ban on illegitimate weapons and tactics is disregarded; or, to put it another way, could assent to a violent contest that set aside these restraints on a purely military outcome.

The same considerations apply to the principle of proportionality itself, since it, like the weapons and tactics ban, is designed to keep suffering out of the reckoning of advantage to the greatest extent possible. Sub-state organisations that lack a realistic prospect of gaining a superior position militarily have an interest in drawing upon other factors to force concessions by the use of disproportionately violent attacks, especially if they can count upon their opponents not resorting to the same tactics, whether by way of specific reprisals or more generally. Such tactics are likely, as we shall see shortly, to work partly by inducing terror, as, for example, in indiscriminate bombing without warnings. Yet it should not be thought that no strictly military advantages flow from this. Indeed, were they not to do so we should scarcely have war at all. Rather what we normally witness in such attacks is a combination of military and non-military methods. Devastating the villages and crops of subsistence farmers, for instance, as often happens in African conflicts, not only terrorises but denies sustenance and shelter to an enemy. Some atrocities by one party are deliberately designed to provoke retaliation by the other which alienates sections of the population who then support or are recruited to the forces of the provocateurs. This is itself a military advantage.

The rule of proportionality and its unconditional cousins, however, may be seen as having the effect of restricting tactics to those which confine the measure of advantage to strictly military advantage only. An instructive example here are the prohibitions upon attacks on so-called 'cultural' property which includes religious buildings and historic monuments.[11] Now evidently the reason for such laws is not the prevention of suffering per se. But it is equally evident that attacking such targets will seldom be of purely military benefit. British bombing in World War II was often deliberately aimed at towns of historic and cultural importance, especially to the Germans, and the German 'Baedecker' raids on English cathedral cities were a reply in kind. The blowing up of mosques and churches by one side or the other in Bosnia is a recent and even more obvious example of what is intended. This is not only the demoralisation of the enemy, since, by the mechanisms we explored in the previous chapter, such blows to national pride can have quite other and easily foreseeable consequences. Rather the point of attacks on an opponents' cultural property is to force them to take account of factors that are not purely military in their assessment of the balance of advantage in hostilities. It is, for example, to force them to see that they risk the loss of their most important symbols of identity.

One way of viewing the rules against such attacks, and, less directly, the rule of proportionality, is as serving to keep the politics of identity *out* of war, so that war becomes a contest in which the military participants could, in principle, engage on morally equal terms, in the sense that neither is advantaged or disadvantaged by the ethical concerns – or lack of them – of their particular culture. One side will not be disadvantaged by, say, its special veneration for its historic sites, or advantaged by metaphysical beliefs that set comparatively little store on life in this world rather than the next. For only if provisions of this kind are in place can soldiers be expected to adhere rigidly to the performance of their role rather than to step outside it and become representatives of their identity groups. If identity considerations can, by these means, be excluded as much as possible from war then so too, if I am right, will many of the horrors of new wars.

The lesson for forces against whom the rules of proportionality are violated is not to be drawn into similar tactics, which will only be taken to legitimise the original breaches and, by alienating their victims, drive them deeper into the camp of extremists. This is, however, unlikely to be the principal temptation of the side that has military superiority, especially if this consists in the kind of technological advantage represented by better airpower or artillery. For then there is likely to be a demand for bombing or bombardment of the enemy which, even if not classifiable as indiscriminate, will result in much greater loss to enemy combatants and non-combatants as well as collateral damage to utilities and so forth than would have resulted from closer engagement of troops. The motive, of course, is to minimise casualties on one's own side. Yet the rule of proportionality requires troops to take risks themselves in order to minimise suffering overall. If this is not done then the restraint in the application of force prescribed by the rule will not have been shown. Nothing is more resented nor is more likely to provoke outright breaches than tactics of this sort adopted by a militarily superior power. That resentment, however, springs from the perception that this is not how a soldier's role should be performed, and it is this perception which needs to be cultivated, not rooted out.

Non-combatant immunity

Hague law is only one arm of the humanitarian laws of war; the other is Geneva law, so-called after its codification largely in the various Geneva Conventions which specify the way in which civilians and those no longer actively involved in conflict, like captured soldiers, are to be treated. We shall return to the latter category in the next section. Here we shall discuss the former category of non-combatants, whose immunity to direct attack under Geneva law represents its expression of the traditional *jus in bello* requirement of discrimination, which limits soldiers to tactics which are aimed at killing or otherwise putting out of action other soldiers, not those who do not bear arms or do not otherwise contribute directly to the prosecution of the war. Discrimination is required, then, to ensure that war is a contest between soldiers, and not an unrestricted killing field between peoples, irrespective of their roles.

In new wars, however, as we observed at the outset of the book, it is just such unrestrained killing that we commonly observe. Is this just an aberration, or is it a consequence of the kind of causes for which they are fought? There are many reasons for fearing that the latter is true. For, as outlined in Chapter 2, there are just causes for which some groups fighting what, on the face of it, seem like any other new wars, should resort to violence, namely when they do so for broadly defensive purposes. But other causes, particularly those associated with the claims to legitimacy discussed in Chapter 3, have a different character. They are causes that derive directly, not from the circumstances people are in, but from the identity they take themselves to have – an identity which supposedly makes their current pattern of political organisation illegitimate. There are several reasons why such a cause can lead to direct attacks upon civilians or lesser, but still deplorable, failures to minimise their suffering.

We noticed earlier a distinction between, on the one hand, the modern defensive version of just war theory, which has emerged through the experience of states in trying to square their general duty to protect ordinary citizens from harm with their conviction that war may sometimes be necessary to fulfil this duty, and, on the other, the older punitive version, which sees war as an instrument of punishment for injustices that cannot otherwise be corrected. It is, however, this latter archaic version of the theory that commonly intrudes itself into the thinking of those who fight what they perceive as an unjust – because an illegitimate – regime, or a state allegedly responsible for the injustice of supporting such a regime. In such a case those who are not innocent of such injustices, in the ordinary sense of the term, will be taken to be permissible targets of attack. These will include not only troops but government functionaries, politicians and obvious beneficiaries or supporters of the illegitimate regime, since all of these will be involved in perpetrating the injustice that the attacks are aimed at correcting. Indeed, targeting them, rather than engaging troops alone, may well be a more effective way of ending the regime through increasing the costs of its maintenance or support.

It is for this reason that we often see in campaigns mounted by sub-state groups, and sometimes, for analogous reasons, in the campaigns against them, a policy of political assassination, despite the fact that this is contrary to customary international law.[12] 'It is a principle of civilised government,' as Arthur Griffith, President of the Irish Free State, observed in 1922, following an IRA political killing, 'that the assassination of a political opponent cannot be justified or condoned.'[13] The reason is not hard to seek. It is that statesmen, and political leaders generally, together with their officials and so forth, occupy roles in which they are required to interact with their counterparts, whether allies or opponents, by way of talks and negotiations. This would be quite impossible if each side in a conflict was simultaneously aiming to execute its opponents. Only political extremists, convinced of their own rectitude, could set aside the need for talking by adopting such a policy. But, as we have seen, extremists reject the roles that make such pacific settlements of conflict possible.

Assassination is, however, far from the worst offence against the prohibition on attacking civilians that we witness in new wars. But even when those targeted are just ordinary people the punitive theory may still be in play. For it may be that those targeted are themselves held responsible for the injustice claimed. This can happen in several ways. In one a doctrine of collective responsibility may be presupposed.[14] Where an attack is launched upon civilian members of a state which is taken to be guilty of supporting injustice, as in the destruction of the Word Trade Center on September 11, 2001, it may be justified on the grounds that these were citizens of the state in whose name the policy was carried out. They, then, are to be punished for permitting it. The situation is somewhat more complicated when a separatist group attacks civilians of the state they currently share. Here it is not simply *qua* citizens, but as those citizens supposedly complicit in the injustice, that they are targeted; for if citizens generally were responsible then the separatists themselves would share the blame, from which they take their resistance to absolve them. Once again, though, even if, as must usually be very doubtful, citizens or sections of the citizenry are collectively responsible for injustices, then it is the state or other political organisation that represents them which should be made the object of attack, not they themselves. This is precisely what war accomplishes, and, by its rules, spares citizens as much as possible. To act against them otherwise is to fail to respect the rights their role confers. But if people are not thereby recognised as citizens then the whole supposed justification of targeting them in this capacity collapses.

Often those who target fellow citizens do so more immediately because of their different identity – they attack them simply because they are Serbs rather than Croats, say. In this case it seems that it cannot seriously be maintained that they should be punished, since they are responsible neither for having the identity they do, nor for the acts that those who share their identity may have perpetrated. And yet it is just when peoples' identities are treated as having the ascriptive character of ethnicity, rather than the putatively voluntary one of political association, that attacks designed to eliminate them or drive them out are most common; and they are carried out in a spirit of indignation. What is presupposed is that the ethnic group or nation itself is responsible, and its members must individually bear the blame. Yet such a view can arise only on the wilder shores of identity politics; for it assumes not only that people must identify themselves with their ascriptive group, but also that in doing so they cannot avoid taking an individual responsibility for the group's actions, past as well as present. To engage in this kind of politics is inevitably to imperil ordinary folk, and it is just this kind of politics which the ban on targeting civilians aims to exclude from military conflict.

Lastly, for our present purposes, but not least notoriously in recent new wars, civilians are attacked because they have the wrong sort of identity for living where they do. The claim is that the current pattern of political organisation is illegitimate in that a certain territory should belong exclusively to the attackers, or that it is legitimate but its legitimacy risks being successfully challenged by others who have come to occupy the territory. In either case the exclusive right of the attackers to the territory is asserted, their attacks constituting the removal of trespassers, with various degrees of violence. It should go without saying that claims to territorial sovereignty are quite distinct from claims to the occupation of property,[15] but this distinction seems to escape ethnic nationalists determined to live only among their own kind. International law, however, forbids the displacement of the civilian population during internal conflicts, except for reasons of security;[16] and rightly so, for if there were to be such a transfer of peoples it should properly come as a result of negotiations to end a properly conducted war, not itself comprise an aspect of hostilities with no military purpose.

We should notice, though, that the permission to move people for their own security or for reasons of military necessity is very easily abused. The commonest use for it in new wars will be to deny shelter to guerrillas and thus create free fire zones; it follows that the people displaced will be those regarded as hostile, so that there may be other motives for forcing them from their homes. That said, the fact that guerrillas operate from among the civilian population poses a problem for their opponents, but it is one easily exaggerated. It is quite wrong to argue, for example, that guerrilla tactics are themselves contrary to the rules of war since they deliberately put civilians in danger by relying upon the scruples of their opponents for their own protection.[17] This is so only if guerrillas are actually fighting from positions occupied by civilians, and certainly it is against the laws of war to locate military objectives among civilian habitation or otherwise use civilians as cover.[18] But this is not the characteristic scenario. Rather guerrillas live among civilians, melting in among them when not fighting. Yet this no more makes civilian centres proper military objectives than would the fact that soldiers on leave live in ordinary undefended towns make them fit targets for bombing. The removal of civilians, then, to combat guerrillas is usually as much for the convenience of isolating political activists from their support base as for the necessity of achieving military objectives. In new wars it is, that is to say, as likely to be on account of their identity that civilians are displaced as because of the hindrance to strictly military operations they create. It is also likely to spread despondency or terror.

Terrorism

New wars are asymmetric, not only in the sense that they originate in conflicts between sub-state insurgents and the regular forces of states, but also in that such conflicts typically involve a great disparity in the amount and sophistication of military force available to each side. The same sort of disparity also typically pertains where external powers intervene against repressive states, as we shall observe in the next chapter. A consequence of this disparity is, of course, that the militarily weaker side has little chance of obtaining victory by conventional military conflict, however justified its cause may be. There are several possible avenues open to it. One is to use the guerrilla tactics which we have just been discussing, denying its adversary the advantages of technological superiority, so long as the rules of war are obeyed and civilians are not exposed to indiscriminate or disproportionate assaults. Such tactics depend upon the support of the local population, and this is sometimes achieved by deliberately provoking such assaults or by other unscrupulous devices. But where support comes of its own accord there is no reason in principle why a guerrilla conflict should not conform to the rules of war and its irregular participants occupy the role of soldiers punctiliously.

This does not necessarily prevent an established state categorising such insurgents as 'terrorists'. One of the reasons for this is that in non-international conflicts states have considerable discretion under international law in how they treat armed opposition personnel. The law maintains that they should be accorded the same status as in international conflicts if they are under proper command and capable of sustained military operations, rather than merely sporadic ones.[19] Most importantly they must themselves display a propensity to abide by the rules of war. Yet it is up to individual states to determine whether these conditions are met and they are usually unwilling to concede that they are, for reasons we shall shortly consider. The result is that their opponents are treated, not with the respect due to combatants which is expressed in, for example, the protections of prisoner of war status, but rather with the odium that disloyalty and criminality attract. 'Terrorists' they will be called, but what, we should ask, is terrorism, for the term is a notoriously unstable one?[20]

One kind of account starts from the idea that terrorism is a species of tactic that insurgents may adopt when they lack the strength or support to launch a guerrilla war. Unable or unwilling to engage enemy troops, they attack or kidnap civilians, engage in sabotage and so forth. An instructive case here is that of Chechnya, the Russian autonomous republic which declared its independence in 1991 and which has been subjected to repeated attempts at suppression by central government forces ever since. During some periods Chechens have been able to mount effective guerrilla resistance but at others they have resorted to less salubrious tactics; throughout they have been branded terrorists on that account, distinguished, supposedly, from Russian forces, by their preparedness to attack civilians for purely tactical reasons and hence not to be bound by the rules of war. What makes fighters terrorists, on this account, is their unscrupulous violation of these rules. They are, that is to say, acknowledged to be fighting a war but they forfeit a military status through breaking war's rules. They are, therefore, confronted principally by a military response but are denied the protections afforded to those whose actions overall constitute in a recognisable way the performance of a soldier's role.

Another kind of account of terrorism treats it simply as the commission of crimes – murder, hijacking, large scale destruction of property and so forth – for political ends, more specifically the sorts of political ends for which people might fight a war, namely revolution, secession and the like. The supposed purpose of such crimes is to achieve these ends not by tactics akin to and often, as in the Chechen case, continuous with military ones, albeit tactics which work largely through demoralising the opposition. It is, instead, to work more directly upon civilians, without necessarily appearing to them at all as a fearful quasi-military presence, namely by depriving them of security and fostering apprehension. This is achieved through such dramatic criminal acts as bombings in city centres which the civil authorities are shown to be powerless to prevent. The confidence of citizens is then sapped. The right response of government, then, is to restore security by a rigorous use of the criminal justice system, supported by the use of troops in aid of the civil power but without the use of the tactics that might be employed in war. On this account campaigns against terrorism, however it is motivated, do not constitute new wars.

One should, of course, treat the kind of account one gives of a general phenomenon, like terrorism, and the forms the phenomenon can take in different circumstances quite distinctly. But the reason for running the enquiries together, as I have done in the preceding two paragraphs, is to bring out the fact that the term 'terrorism' is a multi-purpose pejorative which can be applied to a variety of cases of impermissible violence and to defend a number of different strategies of response. What these responses should be will evidently depend upon what the violent acts are and how it is judged best to counter them. Thus when one sort of response is decided upon terrorism is likely to be characterised in one way, when another then in another way. Thus there is, perhaps, a rough correlation between the rather different violent tactics described in the preceding two paragraphs and the different responses to them indicated there. Yet this is at most an accidental correlation, for what really decides the response is not the nature of the tactics themselves but the sort of threat they pose to a state against which they are directed. Broadly speaking, if it is the sort of threat a war would pose then war is the required response; if not then criminal justice should suffice. But the nature of the tactic will generally indicate the extent of the threat.

Confronted with the superior power of states, sub-state groups may, at least initially, be unable to launch a campaign of a sort that could properly be called war. Yet they still seek the kind of political objectives that war is usually necessary to produce, namely changes to the constitutions or policies of states that they perceive as adversely affecting them. They still intend the violent acts they perform to have the effects of war, and they will, in this sense, think of themselves as waging war, even though they depart from the rules whose general observance is constitutive of a specifically military conflict. They intend to achieve the effects of war by influencing the civilian population of the state, through demoralisation, terrorisation or whatever, into supporting concessions to them. This will be a particularly easy option if the civilian population targeted is itself regarded as the enemy, as in the new war scenario. So long as the state believes that it can limit this influence upon its civilians by preserving security through policing tactics it will rely on a criminal justice response, since it does not yet confront the sort of threat that war poses. But when it does not believe that it can, then it will be forced into a military response with a view to raising the costs of terrorism to unacceptable levels.

The calculation of the level of security required to prevent civilians giving way to terrorists is a political one. No absolute measure of what is due to civilians is presupposed, only of what is required given their level of support for state policies or sympathy for the state's opponents. In some circumstances, then, a criminal justice response may offer less protection than a military one, but a military response may not be made because policing tactics are adequate to the government's purposes. For a military response is inherently a risky one. It reveals that the state is under threat and that its security is fragile. It thereby lends credibility to the terrorists who, overtly at least, seek this sort of response. This may greatly increase their support, especially if the military response targets potential supporters or those with whom they can readily identify. That level of support may rise to the point where more clearly military methods can be employed and even to that where their degree of organisation and operational effectiveness obliges the state to treat them as soldiers and not as mere criminals, and that is as much as to say not as terrorists at all.

The dilemma facing the state, as I have posed it, of whether to opt for a military or a criminal justice response to terror, presupposes that the state's purpose is indeed to protect its citizens. That is to say, that if its response is military then it will be regarding its actions as defensive. In those circumstances its opponents will be viewed as an attacking force to be defeated by military means and, therefore, to be treated no differently from any other enemy troops. Like other enemy troops they forfeit their privileges as combatants if they breach the rules of war, but they are not otherwise to be viewed as criminals. It was a surprise to many observers, then, that America's opponents in the War on Terror – where the description 'war' is evidently to be taken literally – have all along been viewed as criminals. How can they be both criminals to be brought to justice and fighters to be defeated in war?

The apparent paradox evaporates if we accept, as I argued in Chapter 1, that the War on Terror should be thought of as an attempt to wage a punitive just war. For a punitive war is waged against wrongdoers and its purpose is to deliver justice. War is not waged as an alternative to criminal justice, but as a form of it, so that those against whom it is waged can properly be viewed as criminals. The result of so viewing them, however, is to deprive them of the respect due to those whom one engages on equal terms as fellow soldiers, albeit enemies. Several incidents in the War on Terror have illustrated this. America's allies in Afghanistan, the Northern Alliance under General Dostum, treated the Taliban as fellow soldiers and accepted their surrender at Musar-i-Sharif on these terms. But when the Taliban realised that the Americans intended to treat them as criminals they revolted at the Qala-i-Jangi fortress and were subjected to enormous losses. While the Northern Alliance had preserved a traditional politics of role across ethnic boundaries, the Americans denied a military status to their captives even though there was no longer a threat to them, and insisted on pursuing the supposed path of justice.

Statesmen are faced with hard choices when confronting terrorists, but they need to be reminded that their main duty is to safeguard the security of their citizens, not to carry through policies founded on fantastical notions of a national or supranational mission or unfounded claims of national or supranational legitimacy. We shall return to these points in the final chapter. The military power possessed by an established state may tempt it to extremism, though it should not license it. For extremism is manifest not only in acts of terrorism but in the refusal of the powerful to engage in a normal politics of negotiation and conciliation that often provokes violence. But if a military response is decided upon, that again should be calculated in a way that leaves it open to sub-state opponents to conform to the requirement of a military role. Actions which do not, by, for example, creating a relatively risk-free environment for state forces, are themselves liable to drive the desperate or the fanatical to violent extremes. If they are permitted the dignity of the military role, however, they have a reason to avoid those extremes. The right response to extremism, then, must be, wherever possible, to return its adherents to moderation, not to force them further from it.

Notes

1. The key defender of 'trimming' is George Savile, Lord Halifax: see W. Raleigh, *Complete Works of George Savile* (Oxford: Clarendon Press, 1912).
2. *Pace* Theodore Adorno, *The Authoritarian Personality* (New York: Norton, 1969).

3. See Noel O'Sullivan, *Fascism* (London: Dent, 1983), pp. 34–7.
4. J.A. Fisher (who introduced Dreadnoughts), quoted Leslie C. Green, *The Contemporary Law of Armed Conflict* (Manchester: Manchester University Press, 2000), p. 17 fn.
5. Cp. A.J. Coates, *The Ethics of War* (Manchester: Manchester University Press, 1997), ch. 2.
6. Leo Tolstoy, *Essays from Tula* (London: Sheppard Press, 1948), pp. 218, 221.
7. Cp. Hilaire McCoubrey, *International Humanitarian Law* (Aldershot: Ashgate, 1998), pp. 253–7.
8. Quoted W.L. La Croix, *War and International Ethics* (Lanham: University Press of America, 1988), p. 273. (Nechayev was the original of Verkhovensky in Dostoevsky's *The Possessed*.)
9. *Pace* W.L. La Croix, *War and International Ethics*, p. 274.
10. See A.P.V. Rogers, *Law on the Battlefield* (Manchester: Manchester University Press, 1996), ch. 2.
11. See A.P.V. Rogers, *Law on the Battlefield*, ch. 5.
12. See Leslie C. Green, *The Contemporary Law*, pp. 144–5.
13. D. Mercer (ed.), *Chronicle of the 20th Century* (London: Longmans, 1988), p. 296. Note that though the target was an English Field Marshal the targeting of *any* specific individual is a forbidden practice under customary law.
14. For discussion see Burleigh Taylor Wilkins, *Terrorism and Collective Responsibility* (London: Routledge, 1992).
15. See my *The Philosophy of Nationalism* (Boulder: Westview, 1998), ch. 6.
16. See Leslie C. Green, *The Contemporary Law*, p. 326.
17. *Pace* Michael Walzer, *Just and Unjust Wars* (New York: Basic, 1977), p. 286.
18. See Leslie C. Green, *The Contemporary Law*, p. 159.
19. See Hilaire McCoubrey, *International Humanitarian Law*, pp. 25 ff.
20. For extended discussion see my *Terrorism, Security and Nationality* (London: Routledge, 1994), chs 1–4.

6

Righting the Wrongs of War

International society versus cosmopolis

In 1648 the Treaty of Westphalia brought to an end the Thirty Years' War, which had ravaged Europe over those issues of religious identity that have once again surfaced as the occasion of new wars. The system it inaugurated, at least in Europe,[1] was of a society of states, each sovereign in the sense that intervention in its internal affairs was a breach of the society's rules. Such interventions, when the form of coercion applied involves force of arms, constituted aggression, against which states had an absolute right to defend themselves. The system has persisted and been generalised, so that the principle of non-intervention is the cornerstone of the United Nations Charter.[2] It has two purposes. The first is to create a presumption against the use of force as a means of settling international disputes; the second, to create protected spaces within which people can work out their own political arrangements, free of external interference.[3] A condition of membership of international society is that a polity satisfies this latter requirement, at least in theory: colonies are thereby excluded, and so too should be those other political organisations where sections of people lack the status of citizens.

The important point about non-intervention is that there is no reason to think of it as depending upon any general moral principles. For example, it need not be thought of, on the one hand, as protecting the freedom of individuals in accordance with a liberal conception, by providing them with a suitable form of political organisation; nor, on the other, as safeguarding the benefits that flow from communal autonomy, on a communitarian account.[4] To look for such justification is, perhaps, to look in the wrong place and, indeed, to risk importing into the specification of conditions for membership of international society particular disputable moral conceptions. Instead, we should take seriously the fact that the principle's origins and continuing normative force lie in treaties – in agreements to secure or maintain peace; albeit that the original treaty was one that, as it transpired, constituted the parties as able to enter into the kind of relationship to which particular inter-state treaties give a specific shape. What the Treaty of Westphalia did, then, was to make certain kinds of ethical relationship possible by constituting political entities part of whose raison d'être is the avoidance of war and, hence, whose conduct is to be judged by their success or failure in achieving this. To look beyond this for a further justification of non-intervention is to overlook its crucial primary purpose in maintaining peace between states.

Nor should any general ethical justification for seeking peace be expected, as against such other goals as global justice. For the emergence and sustaining of a society of sovereign states rests upon treaties made in particular historical circumstances with their background of recent war and threat of its recurrence. The institutions created and sustained are intelligible only within such a context. They are not, for no human institution could be, shaped with a view to answering all the demands that might conceivably be made upon them, but only to cope with those that have been. This does not, of course, mean that they are immune to change or criticism. It does, however, mean that such critical change must come from within, in the sense that it is a response of those who grasp the rules that govern the operation of states to new historical factors. Those who do this act within roles that are shaped by their place within the state system – as statesmen or citizens. It is, as I have argued throughout, the performance of these roles that makes certain kinds of ethical behaviour possible, and what is possible is constrained by the nature of the institutions within which it has a place.

On this account, peace is not to be thought of as a value to be set beside others or derived from them. Rather that it is valued is something that can be inferred from the performance of statesmen and citizens when they act well, that is to say when they conform their behaviour to the requirements of their roles. For a statesman to lead his citizens to war, for example, other than for defensive reasons, is to act badly, not as judged by any overarching standards of whether peace is, in this instance, more valuable than the fruits of war, but by the standards applicable to statesmen; for it is as a statesman that he acts and thus by those standards alone that he must be judged. To act by other standards, to act *ultra vires* as it were, is not just to act badly as a statesman, it is to risk acting unintelligibly, so that we do not know what the action amounts to. We do not know, for example, in what other ways he is prepared to put the citizens he represents at risk, so that if they follow him it is not clear in what capacity they do so. What is likeliest, however, is that they do so as members of a certain identity group, in the anticipation that its values will somehow by achieved by war.

This brings us back, then, to our topic of new wars. While new wars, as we are understanding them, originate in the actions or reactions of sub-state groups and usually involve the forces of an established state within the same territory, it is often not long before third party states intervene, threaten to intervene or are urged to intervene within that territory for a variety of reasons. In this chapter we shall be considering two such reasons: those that relate to the restoration of peace and security, and those aimed at preventing a gross violation of human rights. The question that confronts us is: when and in what manner are such interventions justified, or do they inevitably breach the principles of non-intervention we have just been discussing? For, it will be observed, the hiatus in the principle is that, while it seeks to minimise the resort to force between states, it does nothing to limit its use within them, nor, for that matter, its use by non-state actors. Yet such uses of force are characteristic of new wars and, it will be suggested, it behoves international society to make a suitable response to them, especially if it is consistently to carry through the concern to avert the horrors of war and bring the benefits of peace that brought it into being.

It is at this juncture that we must introduce, as many readers will believe belatedly, the cosmopolitan position which seems to provide an easy answer to these questions. For cosmopolitanism, as we shall understand it,[5] holds that there are certain universal human rights, graspable independently of their particular institutional forms and including at least the right to life, liberty and a settled existence; that people's possession of these rights makes some claim upon others for their protection; and that, therefore, when the rightholder's own state fails in this regard, it is up to others to provide for it. On this cosmopolitan view, then, the rules of international society should hold good only so long as they succeed in the protection of human rights that provide their ultimate justification. To the extent that they do not they need to be modified, so that, in the circumstances of new wars, intervention may be justified, even when under traditional principles it is impermissible. And certainly we must agree that in these circumstances there is not a secure peace anyway. Intervention here does not start wars; it merely introduces a new element into them, an element aimed both at ending them and at mitigating their effects.

For all that, the burden of this chapter will be to oppose the cosmopolitan case for modifying state practice on intervention and to reject the cosmopolitan rationale. We should start, though, by briefly examining the claim that international society already incorporates cosmopolitan ideas,[6] so that the rule of non-intervention is falling into desuetude. The claim is, then, that we even now occupy a global or cosmopolitan community in the sense that people relate to each other as fellow human beings rather than as citizens of particular states, and expect their government to reflect that fact in policies which conform to universally shared values and promote a degree of global justice by pressing for the implementation of human rights. In support of these last points the 1948 UN Universal Declaration of Human Rights is commonly cited. It is, as has often been noted,[7] a reprise of the American Declaration of Independence and Bill of Rights and of the French Déclaration des Droits de l'Homme et du Citoyen more than a century and a half earlier. The drafter of the UN Declaration declined the suggestion by a Chinese delegate that he should study Confucius before producing a text. There is, then, every reason to see it as springing from a specifically Western cultural milieu, rather than as reliably reporting an international consensus. It is safer to regard it as at best 'doubtful whether' any shared culture that does exist 'includes a common moral culture or set of common values' to underpin international behaviour, even if, as cosmopolitans boldly suppose, there are such universal values to be shared.[8]

The other kind of evidence presented for the claim that we already possess at least the rudiments of a common cosmopolitan culture, is that there are emerging norms of international law licensing intervention in defence of human rights, or even that there has long been such a right in customary international law.[9]

It is true that international law is founded not only on treaties but on the practice and principles recognised by 'civilised nations'.[10] Yet what must be looked at in determining the law is not just what states do and the reasons they give for their actions to their own citizens, but what criticisms other states make and the justifications that are offered to them. On this basis it has been concluded that even in respect of intervention to limit 'an overwhelming humanitarian catastrophe ... the doctrine is far from firmly established in international law' or is 'a violation of the rule tolerated for exceptional reasons rather than ... evidence of the formation of a new rule'.[11,12] For intervention publicised as serving such a purpose is generally opposed by many states and has usually been justified to them in terms of a need to establish peace and security, to which end the UN Security Council can authorise action. But intervention to establish security is a form of defensive action that does not violate the general principle of non-intervention and nor does it require any invocation of human rights and hence does nothing to evidence the existence of a global community agreeing to protect them. It depends only upon the old Westphalian imperative of preserving the peace wherever possible as in the interests of all states, rather than evincing any shared values between them. In looking at cosmopolitan defences of intervention, then, we need to consider them as recommendations for better practice in international relations, not as reflections of an existing one.

Humanitarian intervention

Here is an all too common scenario. First, nationalists launch an armed rebellion in some portion of an established state. Second, the state employs repressive measures against members of the population that the nationalists represent.[13] Third, external powers mount, or at least consider mounting, some form of military intervention in the established state on humanitarian grounds. How are we to assess the ethics of such an intervention, remembering that, in the absence of authorisation from the United Nations Security Council, which is unlikely to be forthcoming, such intervention seems contrary to international law since it involves the use of force 'against the territorial integrity and political independence of a state'?[14] Should we adopt the increasingly influential view that, despite such prohibitions,

the existence of borders is not relevant to the moral justification of military intervention to prevent gross human rights
violations?

What I shall term the 'statist' objection to relaxing the principle of non-intervention hinges on the idea that without authority to take military action within the borders of a state, which
they would possess if invited in by its government, interveners
are, whatever their good intentions, acting unjustly. They are engaged in an act of aggression against the state. The cosmopolitan
response is, of course, to assert that where humanitarian intervention is justified the interveners do have authority to use force
to protect human rights, just as it is the state that normally has
it. Thus, just as the state does not think of its military actions
in quelling low level rebellion as war, but rather as the prevention and punishment of crime, so intervention is often similarly
viewed not as war against the state but as a kind of policing operation. Indeed, there is often a kind of Lockean argument that it
is the government of the repressive state that are now the rebels
committing crimes which need to be prevented or punished.[15] So
one way of presenting the contrast is as a dispute over whether
intervention constitutes war, as statists claim, or something different in principle if not in practice, as cosmopolitans do. And
this issue turns precisely on whether there is a right to cross borders to protect rights when the state fails, as cosmopolitans claim,
or there is not.

One way an objection to intervention might be developed is
this. The established state will allege, in the scenario we envisage, that the rebels lack any authority in their resort to force,
for authority to use force within its borders rests solely with the
established state. Intervention, however benevolent in intention,
will constitute support for the rebels and interveners will possess no more authority than rebels do. There are, I believe, two
conflicting conceptions of a state's authority involved in the cosmopolitan and statist positions. The cosmopolitan regards the
authority of the state as dependent principally upon its role in
safeguarding human rights. The principle of non-intervention is
there simply to enable it to fulfil this role, so that is entitled to
defend itself when attacked just because such an attack threatens its people's human rights. If, however, the state fails in its
role then there is no reason not to intervene and no entitlement

of self-defence against intervention which upholds rather than threatens rights.

The statist conception of authority is less straightforward and can, doubtless, take several forms. The contrast I wish to draw here is between the cosmopolitan's purely administrative view of the state, which loses authority through maladministration, and a view of it as a moral entity responsible for jurisdiction over a people. As such it is the source of law for the people within a given territory, so that different jurisdictions may quite properly be expected to be quite diverse, reflecting the varying circumstances to which people have had to adapt. That the fundamental human rights of life, liberty and settled existence mentioned earlier are to be found in states generally may be taken simply to reflect the fact that they are necessary to anything that we would want to call a state, that is to say, an organisation which maintains order by enforcing law,[16] rather than a tyranny, which reduces people to subjection. That such rights are ostensibly universal in states does not, then, need to reflect the existence of some source of law which lies beyond the state and by which its actions are to be judged. The authority of the state depends, rather, upon its fulfilling its jurisdictional role and is, indeed, lost if that is lost. But its right of self-defence is necessary for it to preserve its jurisdiction within a territory; for there could be no system of specific jurisdictions without a general principle of non-intervention across borders. It is along such lines, I believe, that the statist conceives of authority.

There are different consequences of embracing these contrasting conceptions which explain the different attitudes of cosmopolitans and statists to intervention, but before developing them I want to head off an objection that the statist position, as I have sketched it, is either unmotivated or depends for its plausibility upon cosmopolitan assumptions which should lead all the way to the cosmopolitan conception. The objection is that the statist conception presents jurisdictional rule as preferable to tyranny only because the former safeguards human rights while the latter violates them, so a full blooded cosmopolitanism is the natural conclusion to draw. But this objection simply begs the question: Why should we not say instead that human rights are valued, not as independently identifiable goods, but as aspects of living under jurisdictional government? Their value is simply

inferable from the fact that they are respected by those who are
happy to perform a citizen's role appropriately.

Let us turn, then, to the sorts of way an external power might
respond to a state's denial of their authority to intervene, and
see whether these are best made sense of on a cosmopolitan or a
statist conception. As will now be obvious, what such a power
must do is claim that the state intervened in has lost its authority
in the relevant respect. The authority of external powers cannot,
therefore, be attacked as trespassing upon the state's authority
but rather derives from alternative sources in the absence of it.
This response admits of a number of different versions depending both upon its theoretical grounding and on the particular circumstances prevailing. Analytically it is important to distinguish
several cases even though in practice they may be composited or
confused.

The first is that in which authority is lost because the established state can no longer control a part of its territory so that
there is a breakdown of law and order within it. In this case
another state may justify intervening as required to maintain
order and thereby prevent the violation of human rights which
may result from disorder. Assuming that the intervening power
does have some authority in such a case,[17] it is important to
see that the scope of this sort of justification is quite restricted.
Few cases of intervention have this structure. In most, disorder
is only a temporary effect of civil strife, not a chronic condition
requiring this sort of action. Indeed, we should be careful not
to exaggerate the extent of cases of breakdown of authority by
assimilating to them situations in which a state is acting to put
down insurgency. Since the state needs such powers to maintain
its jurisdiction it cannot lose its authority just because it must
use coercive measures to restore jurisdictional ones.[18]

I want to contrast cases of a breakdown of authority with
those that are more typically exemplified in our scenario, namely
where the established state supposedly forfeits its own authority
because of its repressive behaviour. Two different claims could
be involved here and they must be distinguished. The first is that
the state forfeits authority globally, that is, across the whole of its
territory, rather than, as in the second claim, only locally, that is,
only in a part. The first claim could be argued for on the grounds
that it behaves so badly throughout, and not just in a part of,
its territory that its claim to exercise authority no longer holds

good anywhere. This is not the situation in our scenario where only a portion of the population is badly treated. But here too an argument for global forfeiture of authority can be made, rather than for merely local forfeiture in that part of the territory where the badly treated portion lives.

The case is made by claiming that a state which grossly violates its subjects' human rights loses its title to political authority because this depends precisely upon its upholding their rights. For a state's upholding their rights gives citizens some reason to accept its commands as in their general interest and thereby to recognise the state as having authority and not just power. If it acts otherwise then people *qua* citizens, rather than *qua* members of the dominant group which is not mistreated, have no reason to obey its injunctions just because it is the state which issues them. Intervention in such a state, it may be suggested, cannot trespass upon an authority the state has lost by its own bad behaviour. The intervener's own authority derives from its acting to protect citizens just as a properly functioning state should do and which, indeed, gains its authority precisely by so doing.

Now this, it seems to me, is the position which a cosmopolitan is likely to espouse, for *qua* administrative unit the state has failed in its duty to protect human rights and has, in fact, violated them. That this has been of only local effect does not alter the fact that the state forfeits its office in this regard so that others may perform it. That it continues to protect rights over the rest of its territory does not affect the issue. Indeed, it only reveals its partiality and consequent failure to grasp the moral purpose, and hence universal application, of human rights. The natural corollary of this global forfeiture of authority is that a change of regime is needed, and that is just what numerous contemporary interventions set out to achieve, so that their work is done when a more enlightened regime which does protect human rights is in place. Such a view resembles older ideas of the right to depose tyrants. But, I shall argue, those ideas do not consort well with the cosmopolitan picture of what humanitarian intervention should be like in our scenario.

We need to remember that in our scenario there is a civil war or something close to it. In these conditions coercion is the order of the day and its permissible limits are unclear. They cannot include, though, outrages against the civil population which would be contrary to the rules of war in international conflicts. Suppose such outrages were to occur there. Then there might be an analogous case for humanitarian action in such an international conflict as in a domestic one. But here, it would seem, we would have no special kind of action, detached from the main conflict. Rather, we would witness an entry into it on the side of those who principally suffer. Such alliances are, of course, not what the cosmopolitan envisages. For she thinks of her sort of intervention as essentially unmediated by such a relation to a warring party, but rather as the introduction of a third party with the distinct and limited agenda of safeguarding human rights, and as such not really war at all. Yet it is unclear why a domestic differs from an international conflict in this regard, and if the cosmopolitan picture is implausible for the latter then it is implausible for the former too. The upshot of these considerations is, I suggest, that humanitarian intervention in our scenario cannot credibly be viewed as action on behalf of the whole population of the state intervened in, with a change of regime the solution to their problems. It is inevitably slanted towards aiding the repressed part of the population. Its authority is, on a statist account, to be sought in its relation to that part, as we shall now go on to see.

It should not be thought that statists cannot contemplate the possibility that some rebellions are justified. After all, many states, perhaps most, are the products of rebellion. What may justify rebellion is the forfeiture of the established state's authority locally rather than globally, namely in respect of that part of its population whose human rights it is violating. For suppose the state is repressing a national or other minority in its territory. Then it seems natural to say that it forfeits authority over them specifically, since the fact that it does not treat them like other citizens as benefiting from the protection of the law releases them from the normal obligations they have to it. The state retains its authority over those who enjoy jurisdictional governance, and loses it over those who do not. And on this kind of account authority over the latter will pass to an opposition body willing and able, in principle, to exercise jurisdiction in their part of the territory.

It is because authority over a part of the established state's original territory passes to another political organisation in that part that external military assistance to secure this transition need not be thought to breach the principle of non-intervention which statists wish to uphold. For the external power will typically recognise a new state in that part so that, in its eyes, intervention in the established state's territory has not occurred. While we may continue to think loosely of external assistance in this situation as intervention, as doubtless it will be so thought of by the established state and perhaps even in current international law, it is important to see that on statist principles it does not have to be so regarded and, if its true character is properly grasped, is better not. Thus, permitting external assistance does not require a change in international law which permits intervention within a state.[19] For it allows the preservation of the principle of sovereignty while still permitting military aid to repressed groups, thus escaping between the horns of the dilemma that we either recognise state sovereignty or protect people from injustice. It is true that the territorial integrity of an existing state may be breached, but so it is whenever a secession is recognised. What sort of situation, though, would justify external assistance for a rebellion?

In the circumstances of our scenario a regime change may not be an adequate remedy for the minority's wrongs. For here what is being suggested is that it is the state itself, not just the regime, which has forfeited authority because its very structure of domination and subordination are what permit the minority to be repressed. Constitutional change is what is needed, and the constitutional changes required to prevent repression may involve redrawing boundaries so that the minority gains a separate state. This is the case I shall concentrate on here because it is theoretically the simplest one. But I want to distinguish two easily confused ways in which the case for secession may be made, one of which, I shall argue, may justify external assistance to achieve it, while the other probably does not.

The first kind of case is this. Authority is lost, as we said, because the minority no longer has obligations to a state which represses it. They lack obligations because acceptance of the state's commands cannot reasonably be expected when these are tyrannical rather than jurisdictional. Indeed, far from being under any obligations the repressed minority has a right to defend itself against the consequences of disobeying tyrannical commands. Insofar as a right of secession is being claimed here, under which authority rightfully passes from one state to another, it depends upon the rights of people to defend themselves when unjustly attacked. In the circumstances they are in they may need to secede to exercise these rights, if only a separate state can protect them. Their right of secession is, therefore, what I have called a 'circumstantial' right.[20] This is very different analytically from allowing, in a second kind of case, what I call, by contrast, a 'systemic' right of secession, that is to say a right which derives not from the circumstances the group finds itself in but from the kind of group it is, for example a national group. Their right of secession, if they have one, would derive from a group of this kind having a right of self-determination.

However, external assistance to secure secession should not be thought of as necessarily aimed at advancing self-determination so understood. It may promote such political separation simply as a defence against human rights violations. It is easy to overlook this when the group whose rights are violated is, by some criterion, a national group and especially when it is a group claiming a systemic right of secession. Indeed, the grounds one may have for thinking that the repressive state's authority over the group is permanently forfeit may be that the state represses them *qua* members of a separate national group, rather than just as any group of rebellious subjects. For if this is the case then their prospects for obtaining just treatment within the existing state may well be remote. The state itself has, by its own behaviour towards them, acknowledged their distinctiveness and implied that it is unprepared to treat them equally with other citizens within a common polity. In these circumstances it is *as* the supposedly national group that a separate political organisation is sought for them. But it is sought *because* members of that national group are mistreated, not because the group is a national one.

Even if all this is true analytically, so that humanitarian actors may, on a statist conception, derive their authority from allying with circumstantially entitled secessionists, the situation on the ground in the scenario we envisage is much less clear cut. The established state will claim that its actions against the minority, even if repressive, are a reaction to a rebellion which it has a right to suppress: they are, that is to say, directed against the minority *qua* rebels, not *qua* their constituting the national group they supposedly do. However, as we saw in our discussion of secession earlier, a history of official repression or even mere serious discrimination, antedating nationalist insurgency, may tell decisively against the state's claim. It is important, however, that external powers should not find themselves manipulated by nationalists who provoke repression in order to generate a humanitarian case for support. Conversely, some repressive re-actions are so massively disproportionate to the threat posed that they can only be interpreted as directed against the minority per se, not against it as a rebellious group. It is in these sorts of circumstance, I am suggesting, that humanitarian action may be rightfully undertaken.

We have in this situation a straightforward case of a minority group engaged in armed conflict with the forces of the established state and which possesses proper authority on account of that state's forfeiture of it through repressive behaviour – behaviour which cannot be explained simply as a reaction to a rebellion for which the rebels lack any authority. Then military action by external powers may involve an alliance with rebels strictly for humanitarian ends and irrespective of the rebels' wider goals. In this case those giving military assistance are engaged in a just war because the self-defence of the national minority is a just cause. But it is a just cause because what is being defended are the individual members of the minority themselves. No reliance is placed, as it would be if systemic rights were involved, on the kind of group the minority constitutes and whether as such it has a claim to be defended.[21]

In such an alliance external powers are fighting a war, the point of which, like that of inter-state war, is to secure a space within which jurisdictional rule can be maintained by those who represent the people there. It is not, unless incidentally, their job to do anything that could properly be called law enforcement or policing to protect human rights. For if those violating rights are the forces of the state then these need to be beaten back militarily. If, by contrast, they are armed gangs under no proper authority then it is the rebel government's responsibility to deal with them, and external forces can only assist in this. They are not, as on cosmopolitan principles, doing some police work on their own authority. Indeed, they would be infringing the authority of their allies were they to do so by operating in accordance with their own conceptions of justice, not those of their allies.

The resistance of cosmopolitans to this statist story is based on the idea that there is no theoretical need for such an internal group to mediate the authority of external agents to protect in-dividual human rights. On just war principles I believe that there is, if only because to go to war justly one must have a just cause.

But if the state offering external assistance has not been wronged then it itself lacks such a cause. It is those on whose behalf it acts who have a just cause, and the assisting state acquires one by allying with them. But it can associate itself with the rebels' cause only if the rebels have authority to fight for it.[22]

Furthermore, the just war account of justifiable military support for a repressed minority seems to me to be much more realistic than the cosmopolitan defence. It grants that external powers will have their own interests and will choose to enter or not to enter alliances accordingly. It presupposes, though this raises larger questions than the present work can address, that humanitarian action is a political option for particular states, rather than the general duty that cosmopolitans take it to be. In exercising this option external powers will, if successful, effect constitutional changes internationally. These affect the shape of political communities, not just the lives of individuals. Inevitably these changes will alter the relationships of relative amity or enmity between states and hence the balance of power. States will intervene on behalf of potential friends, not enemies. They will also be cautious, so as not to provoke counter-intervention, for the fear of alliance with internal groups is always that of internationalising a domestic conflict and turning what is ugly but limited into something ultimately bloodier even if better regulated. Conversely, however, the fear of external action on behalf of secessionists should deter an established state from repressing a minority more than if it could be confident that following any intervention its territorial integrity would be retained.

The cosmopolitan preference, other things being equal, for changing regimes rather than borders depends on its fundamental assumption that human rights can be grasped quite independently of their embedding in any particular type of jurisdiction. As such it requires, in principle, only an enlightened regime to put them into effect. The statist conception, by contrast, goes naturally with a view of human rights as differently understood in the different jurisdictions from which they arise. The moral significance of boundaries is to protect such particular jurisdictions as what make possible a tolerably happy life for those within them. But not just any boundaries can create viable jurisdictions, and that for a whole variety of quite contingent reasons. One reason is the unwillingness of members of some dominant group to treat their fellows as equal citizens, which may, notoriously, have ideological underpinnings in the belief that they are, indeed, not equal. In these circumstances jurisdictional rule for both groups within the same boundaries may not be consistently applied, so that the system does not embed anything that we could think of as human rights. It is such circumstances, I have argued, on statist principles, that may give rise to a justified secession and humanitarian action in support of it.

Peace and security

Not all external interventions in states have humanitarian objectives. Some seem, at least prima facie, simply extensions of the right of self-defence that states have against other states. Not all attacks, however, are launched by states, and not all attacks launched by sub-state actors are directed at the state within which they are located. Some, most notoriously the September 11 attacks with hijacked airliners on the Pentagon and World Trade Center, are directed at states whose foreign policies are contrary to the objectives of sub-state actors based elsewhere. Such objectives can be of various sorts. They include both the defence of some group of people, either in the sub-state actors' home area or abroad, and self-determination for a group, either one occupied or colonised, or one seeking political recognition of its identity. These objectives evidently have different complexions vis-à-vis their providing a just cause of war, whatever the attackers' other qualifications for having a *jus ad bellum*. Furthermore, they relate differently to the state attacked, from those seeking to defend people against direct aggression by that state to those aiming to discourage it from supporting other states deemed illegitimate. The objectives of international sub-state actors are usually mixed, running from ones that involve issues of political concern which warrant proper consideration to those that represent the political vision of small and largely unsupported groups of intellectuals.

What should be the response of the states attacked? Given that many, though not all, attacks by poorly equipped sub-state actors are terrorist operations directed against civilian targets one might expect a primarily criminal justice response, as is usual in the case of domestic terrorism. A number of factors stand in the way of this. One is that if the organisers of the attack are based in a foreign and usually hostile country it will often be impossible to apprehend them and bring them to justice in the ordinary way, leaving the state looking powerless to protect its citizens. Another is that while domestic terrorism usually challenges the legitimacy of the state attacked, which is best asserted by a response which criminalises attackers rather than by treating them as legitimate political actors, no such challenge is usually involved in international terrorism. A third is that the scale of the threat from international terrorism is likely to be greater, since better organisation and resources are required to mount it and a foreign base makes it harder to counter, so that, just as against domestic terrorism which poses a large threat, a war response may be anticipated. Even so, the sub-state actors responded to will, as we saw earlier, still be categorised as criminals rather than as the bona fide belligerents they regard themselves as being.

How, though, should such a war be conducted? Inevitably it will involve armed intervention in the territory of another state which is impermissible except in self-defence or when undertaken under UN auspices for ensuring peace and security. Let us consider the first alternative. This justification is certainly offered for such interventions, as we have already seen, but two sorts of factor need to be borne in mind before accepting it. The first concerns the relationship between international terrorists and the state intervened in. Where this relationship is close, in the sense that terrorists are either acting on behalf of that state or are being given shelter by it, then a self-defensive operation may reasonably be regarded as having the same sort of justification as if it were launched in direct response to an attack by the state itself, for the state is acting wrongfully in permitting the attack. The case is different, however, where terrorists operate outside the control of the state they are based in: is there a right of intervention here, where that state is not acting wrongfully? International lawyers have suggested that this might be justified on grounds of necessity,[23] usually only one ingredient in self-defence, rather than as self-defence itself, which would require the imputation of aggressive behaviour by the state against which defence is sought. The requirements for this are, however, very stringent: viz. that only such an intervention, strictly limited in its scope, can preserve the vital interests of the state attacked.

This brings us to the second sort of factor relevant to armed intervention against an international terrorist threat. A defensive military operation must be both necessary and proportionate, that is to say, such as is required to counter a current threat of sufficient magnitude to constitute an armed attack and no more. There is controversy amongst the international lawyers as to whether it can go beyond that and serve as a deterrent to future terrorist attacks, so that it is to this extent pre-emptive.[24] As we have already seen, however, what is clear is that to count as defensive, armed intervention must not be punitive. It cannot, that is to say, constitute a form of punishment for terrorist acts for which ordinary criminal sanctions are not available. Evidently this is the character that many responses to international terrorism do have, and as such they cannot be regarded as involving permissible interventions in another state. Such action is open to objections against intervention which represents itself as a form of police action, whether against the terrorists themselves or against the state that harbours them. The only action which could fairly be so represented is that which is aimed at enforcing international law. But violating international law is scarcely a method of upholding it, for a high-handed moralism is precisely what often motivates the terrorists themselves. As always, it is policies to secure compliance on all sides that should be looked for if peace and a reasonable redress of grievances are aimed at.

There is, in any case, a peculiar danger in waging war against international terrorist groups which must be mentioned. While domestic terrorists are commonly extremists pursuing by force of arms policies which significant numbers of people in their area already support, international terrorists are often 'vanguardists', in the sense that they seek to build support for their preferred policies by actions intended to elicit a military response and thus to polarise people into friends and enemies. The actions of Pan-Islamic groups appear to be of just this sort. While a common Islamic identity is acknowledged by Muslims in many countries, so that attacks on co-religionists by those of a different faith may be resented, this is as yet a long way from the desire to restore the common political identity once represented by shared submission, at least by Sunnis, to the Caliphate of Baghdad, an office assumed, until their collapse, by the Sultans of the Ottoman Empire. Yet Pan-Islamic groups intend to effect this transformation by placing themselves in the vanguard of a revolutionary struggle to destabilise existing state boundaries by luring Western states into confrontation with a variety of largely Muslim states. They aim to build a Pan-Islamic nation from the outside in, so to speak, by first providing its political and military organisation, rather than allowing these to emerge from inside a pre-existing body of those with Pan-Islamic political aspirations. The danger of war in this kind of case is, then, to boost support for a particular manifestation of identity politics; its consequences may be much graver than the original attack that sparked the war.

It should not be thought, however, that a Pan-Islamic political identity necessarily creates greater dangers than any other sort, except perhaps in its scope for destabilising existing structures (which is, incidentally, no worse than that of the break-up of the Soviet Union). There is good reason to worry here that an attack on Pan-Islamists merely manifests a Western preference for states founded on voluntarist principles around shared characteristics like language and history over a culturally different principle of a political organisation. Such a preference is quite distinct from a commitment to forms of organisation that treat all the inhabitants of a state as equal citizens, however they identify themselves – a commitment that largely Muslim states have often, through various devices, been able to fulfil.[25] It is a challenge to this commitment, not a rejection of liberalism, that arguably poses a threat to peace and security in some situations, and this brings us to the role of United Nations' sponsored actions mentioned earlier as providing a second alternative for justifiable interventions against international terrorism.

Some humanitarian interventions have been justified as meeting threats to peace and security when following, though not always directly authorised by, Security Council resolutions. There is a risk that such justifications come to mirror general views about what sorts of behaviour constitute threats rather than specific concerns about a particular political situation. So it is in the case of the idea that terrorism per se is the kind of threat to international peace and security that calls for collective action under UN authorisation. 'Security' is, literally, freedom from care, that is, from the anxieties that would prevent people from engaging in those relationships with each other that are regulated by government. The maintenance of security is the preservation of such a social order against threats to dissolve it. The responsibility to achieve this in respect of domestic terrorism rests with individual governments. Where they lack the power to do so then this is likely to be because they do not command sufficient popular support, and security may best be assured by, for example, conceding the claims of insurgents, rather than resisting them. It can, in general, be no business of other states to interfere, whether through international bodies or otherwise.

How does the case of international terrorism differ from this? The difficulties facing a state under such attack in responding effectively within international law may suggest that actions to provide collective security under explicit UN authorisation are called for. The purpose of such operations is, in the first place, to give assistance to the victims of aggression and to prevent the escalating violence to which unilateral action may lead. Attacks by international terrorists may require such a collective response – a response which will always have the preservation of peace and the restoration of security as its main objectives, so that force will be a last resort, to be employed reluctantly, without the vengeful motivations of the victims themselves. The effectiveness of such a response requires, of course, a genuine commitment to peace, which is inconsistent with a propensity to exploit the situation that evokes it for particular political ends.

No doubt there is an element of idealism here, but the thinking behind such collective security arrangements should not be confused with cosmopolitanism. It is not that international agencies are taking on the work of states which can no longer guarantee the security of their citizens against attack; for it is states which are being assisted in carrying out their obligations, not relieved of them. Still less should cosmopolitan ideas be permitted to cloud the point of collective security operations against international terrorist groups, which is to restore security, that is to say, to restore a situation in which order can be maintained through the enforcement of the law. It is not to be confused with the kind of international law enforcement activities that cosmopolitans envisage, since the securing of space within which the law can be enforced is one thing, enforcing it is quite another. As in the case of humanitarian intervention the policing analogy for collective operations against international terrorists is quite inappropriate. For, insofar as they are guilty of criminal offences and lack the immunity of combatants, trial within the appropriate jurisdiction is the proper remedy, not war (which paradoxically provides them with a case for claiming such immunity).

Yet cosmopolitan notions do seem to affect views of what action against international terrorism amounts to in just these sorts of ways. This can be seen in the moralising conception of it as aimed at removing not simply some specific and localised danger but a general and pervasive threat to 'civilised values' or the like, that is to say the sorts of values which, on a cosmopolitan account, underpin the human rights that terrorists supposedly hold in contempt. It is, however, quite unclear what a war against terrorism and in support of such values could possibly amount to. Is it armed action by sub-state actors per se that is objected to as somehow a threat to human rights? Surely not, for sometimes such action is undertaken to defend them. Is it specifically sub-state action across international boundaries? This too is sometimes claimed to be defensive and not without reason. Is it sub-state action that destabilises the borders within which law and order can be maintained? Again not, as there is a wider tolerance, on broadly liberal principles, of self-determinative struggles which have this effect than might otherwise seem desirable. Is a war against terrorism, then, morally continuous with humanitarian interventions to protect civilians against a repressive state regime – a campaign against gross violation of human rights wherever perpetrated? Tempting as this comparison is,[26] it too should be rejected. Not only is the scale of civilian fatalities resulting from terrorist action, even on September 11, small by comparison with that which usually prevails when humanitarian intervention is canvassed, so it is not loss of life itself that is the main concern; it is the threat to security that springs from it. It is as yet, however, the effective working of the state system which provides this security, not some untried cosmopolitan alternative.

War crimes trials

Interventions by external states, whether humanitarian or defensive, often aim also at apprehending and bringing to trial the members of offending regimes, both political and military, or terrorists sheltering under them. On the cosmopolitan principles which are often invoked to support interventions this is a natural corollary of their international policing character. Certainly there is scope for international justice, as meted out in international courts and tribunals set up under UN auspices. But we need to inquire into its rationale, without the facile assumption that it is simply a means of enforcing some universal standards of morality. For, as such, any particular international proceedings are likely to be objected to by defendants as imposing standards that they themselves conscientiously reject, believing, as they do, that in their particular circumstances their acts were morally justified. Perhaps it is possible to exaggerate the extent of such grievances and admit that many of those charged with international crimes know that what they do is wrong even by their own lights.[27] Yet it is important that international justice should not have the appearance of imposing moral standards that others cannot acknowledge, especially if these are the standards of the victors in some armed conflict. Its importance requires, then, a rationale independent of such moral standards whose source is, like the source of any putatively universal morality, obscure.[28]

The suggestion that flows most obviously from the argument of this book is that where people are put on trial before international courts or tribunals the purpose should be to provide sanctions for the proper performance of their roles, where these are not available through the operation of ordinary domestic law. The International Criminal Court, set up in 1998, has jurisdiction with respect to four sorts of crime: genocide, crimes against humanity, war crimes, and the crime of aggression (to be added as soon as it can be adequately defined – though in the form of 'crime against peace' it was one of the offences for which the Nazis were tried at Nuremberg). This last, together with genocide and crimes against humanity, are principally, though, not exclusively the sorts of crime that statesmen, political leaders, and officials might be tempted to commit, while war crimes, in the narrow sense of violations of the laws of war governing *jus in bello*, are mainly the crimes of soldiers. We may construe the Court's proceedings, then, and those of the ad hoc tribunals which preceded it, as established to regulate the performance of statesmen and the like, on the one hand, and of soldiers, on the other, where this cannot be otherwise controlled. They are an expression of international society's demands, in the former case, upon those who represent its members and analogous groups, in the latter, upon those who fight for them.

International aggression is a clear case of an offence against these rules which no merely domestic jurisdiction could be expected to handle fairly. Yet equally it will, in particular cases, be a politically contentious matter whether offensive military action constitutes aggression, which no purely legal tribunal, however impartial, could be expected to adjudicate upon in any but the most flagrant instances. It is precisely such controversial cases to which comprehensive peace settlements are better fitted than legal proceedings, since they command the agreement of both sides, however recriminatory. The same goes for internal attacks that could be dealt with only by domestic law, which might, in the interests of peace, be suspended with advantage, as we shall go on to see. Genocide and crimes against humanity more generally are also unlikely to be handled satisfactorily by domestic courts. They will not be where they arise from deep divisions of an ethnic or political character that are unresolved at the time of court proceedings, which will then reflect either vengefulness on one side – such as led the Rwanda Tutsis to insist on executing Hutus – or exculpation on the other – as in legal actions against senior army personnel proving abortive in many South American countries.

It is better, however, that even such grave crimes should be dealt with domestically if they can be adjudicated upon impartially, since whatever other wrong their perpetrators have committed they have wronged their own state – both by failing to treat some of its citizens as they have a right to be treated and by failing to represent any of them in the appropriate way. Only a domestic forum may enable citizens to appreciate this and thus to resume their own roles properly. A related reason for preferring national to international justice in such cases is,[29] indeed, that it forces citizens to confront their own part in crimes against their fellows, at home or abroad, for their leaders will seldom be able to commit them without collusion. Only if a trial or other enquiry takes place within their own jurisdiction are they able to see that justice is being done specifically on their behalf, and not in the name of some notional global community.

Yet there are often, it might be objected, insuperable difficulties in bringing such offences as those that count as crimes against humanity before domestic courts. Statesmen will not usually be breaking their country's own laws in committing crimes against humanity. They will probably make sure that the law is adjusted to sanction their inhuman acts. To try them, then, will breach the principle of *nulla poena sine lege* (without a law in force at the time no penalty may fairly be imposed). This was, in fact, part of the defence of those tried at Nuremberg. Yet whatever its other defects, and they are many, Nuremberg was right in this point, as the German jurist of the time, Gustav Radbruch, explained in his famous formula:

> Where justice is not even aimed at, where equality – the core of justice – is deliberately disavowed in the enactment of a positive law, then the law is not simply 'false law', it has no claim at all to legal status.[30]

The point is that where political leaders deviate so flagrantly from the requirements of their role as to appropriate the apparatus of the law for extra-legal ends they are not acting as public role-holders at all, and hence their acts cannot succeed in creating laws. They lose their official character to such an extent that their acts are disallowed as public acts. It is, therefore, quite in order to arraign them for breaches of the laws they have sought to set aside, which proscribe murder, kidnapping and so forth.

As far as war crimes, in the strict sense, of soldiers are concerned, there seems to be a more straightforward case for preferring domestic to international jurisdiction. It is again, however, related to the needs for statesmen and citizens to recognise their own responsibilities in ensuring that those who fight on their behalf do so within the rules of war. While the conduct of junior soldiers will be dealt with through military procedures as part of the maintenance of discipline and good order, that of commanders needs to be scrutinised publicly in order that citizens may realise and accept the limits under which their forces must operate. For, as we have seen, it is only if they think of themselves as citizens rather than as holders of an identity supposedly relevant politically, like ethnicity, that they will appreciate the point of these limitations in countering the uncontrolled violence of hatred and revenge. Direct attacks upon civilians, mistreatment of prisoners and so forth can, at least when passions cool, be seen as unacceptable as readily in a domestic as in an international forum. Indeed, they are simply domestic crimes, in committing which soldiers lose the immunity they possess as combatants.

It has to be conceded, however, that grossly disproportionate acts, which secure military objectives at little cost to a country's combatants but at a great price in terms of the lives of enemy civilians, are unlikely to be recognised for what they are domestically since they are done presumably with the immunity of combatants. Although arguably these are the acts of war in most need of control, it is hard to see that even international tribunals could adjudicate upon them satisfactorily, since the measure of proportionality is ill defined in purely military terms, rather than political ones. None of this is to say that there is no place for international justice, even in the case of war crimes narrowly defined. Soldiers, though answerable in the first instance to statesmen and political leaders, just as they in their turn are answerable to their citizens, are also answerable to their fellows in international society – in the case of soldiers to the military community which historically through custom and latterly through Conventions, have made many of the laws of war by mutual agreement. To violate them is to contravene agreed rules governing relations with fellow soldiers and may need to be marked as such. For while, as noted earlier, the purpose of reprisals during a war is to deter further violations, the aim of post-war proceedings against war crimes must be the re-establishment of the laws of war as regulative of military conduct.

Amnesty

If peace is the real priority in ending wars then, it may be argued, other desirable ends, such as the bringing to justice of those guilty of aggression, war crimes and so forth, may need to be set aside. In the making of peace – indeed to secure peace at all – it may be necessary to offer an amnesty to those who would otherwise be brought to trial, and this is particularly the case in civil conflicts of the sort that typify new wars. Theorists of a cosmopolitan disposition are characteristically mistrustful of such amnesties.[31] After all, they insist, though a state no doubt has the legal right to pardon purely domestic offences, crimes against humanity or peace are international crimes to which perpetrators should be answerable to the whole global community. These rhetorical flourishes do not advance the argument against treating such actions either, where possible, as ordinary crimes against domestic laws that forbid murder and so forth, or as breaches of the rules of international society, to which the perpetrators are answerable to their peers among the political leaders with whom they need to deal. They, too, like states, may be prepared to set aside transgressions in the interests of the peace they are working for.

Amnesties are offered under different conditions in different circumstances. Sometimes they are quite unconditional or conditional only upon the continuation of the peace in return for which they are offered, as in the prisoner release that has been a crucial part of the Northern Ireland peace process. Sometimes this marks a readiness to put the past behind; sometimes merely resignation to the realities of power, as in so many South American states where the military can, and does, overthrow democratic governments.[32] In all these cases considerations of justice give way to the requirement for peace. In other cases, however, amnesties are made conditional upon co-operation with a commission designed to establish the truth about alleged abuses of human rights that took place during the conflict. The main aim here is to secure a reconciliation between the parties to it, and it is a question of political judgement whether such an investigation will serve this end. In respect of Northern Ireland, for instance, the Irish premier, Bertie Ahern, reported his 'assessment that people feel that, on balance, the potential harm that would flow from disclosure, against the background in particular of the small size of the society and of local communities would outweigh the benefits.'[33]

Ahern was speaking on his return from South Africa, whose Truth and Reconciliation Commission (TRC) is the best known example of this kind of process. The Commission was created following the collapse of the apartheid regime, which not only routinely abused human rights but fought a dirty war against its African National Congress opponents. While the TRC has been charged with sacrificing justice to other ends, supporters have denied this, claiming either that it offers a principled compromise between justice and social unity,[34] or that, while not delivering retributive justice, it offers another form – restorative justice.[35] In any case, they argue it dispenses whatever justice is appropriate to the transition South Africa has been undergoing.[36] There are, then, three questions we must address. The first is what exactly the charge of injustice levelled at the TRC amounts to. The second is whether the goals of the TRC, explicit or implicit, are, indeed, those of criminal and civil justice. And the third is how the transitional conditions in which the TRC operate are relevant to the justice it seeks to dispense.

Opponents of the TRC chanted, 'No amnesty, no amnesia, just justice'.[37] Their objection was, in effect, that those granted amnesty in return for appearing before the Commission were getting away scot-free with murder and other crimes. They were also being granted immunity from civil action. Thus the perpetrators were neither punished nor obliged to recompense their victims. The perpetrators did not get their due deserts, and the victims' wrongs went uncorrected. Whatever the *political* justification for this, 'justice would', in Kant's words, 'cease to be justice if it were bartered away for any consideration whatsoever'.[38] That is the charge.

Two distinct principles are operating in the allegation that the TRC does not deliver justice. One is the maximalist version of retributivism which holds that justice is not done unless every crime is punished. The other is the idea that the victim of crime – or his family – has a claim upon the perpetrator. These come together in, and perhaps only in, the view sardonically expressed by Sir James Fitzjames Stephen that 'criminal law stands to the passion of revenge in much the same relation as marriage to the sexual appetite'.[39] The law acts on behalf of the victims and unjustly neglects its duty to them if it fails to prosecute. It is, then, unsurprising that in disavowing retribution as its aim the TRC equated retribution with such institutionalised revenge.

There is not space here to investigate these principles.[40] The point I want to make is a simple one. It is that the charge of injustice concerns the treatment of the perpetrators, and it is made by or on behalf of the victims and their families. It is this charge that must be answered. It is not clear that it can be answered by appeal to a compromise, however principled. For, firstly, a compromise seems to concede that perpetrators do *not* get their due deserts; and, secondly, it is not a compromise *agreed* to by the victims. If it is replied that it is still a fair or just compromise then the response may be that this is an *ignoratio elenchi*. The justice of the compromise is not what is in question: the justice of the treatment of the perpetrators is.

Before conceding the charge of injustice, though, let us glance at what happens when a perpetrator of rights violations is granted amnesty. The bargain the perpetrator strikes is to trade his right of silence for immunity. Now is such a bargain a second best to justice or itself an example of justice in operation? Certainly no retribution is involved, but equally certainly the perpetrator gives something up, so that if the bargain is a fair one then arguably justice is being done. Whether it is fair depends on whether all the relevant parties are properly involved and whether the terms they make are not prejudiced by the use of unequal power (as happened in amnesties granted to the military in South America). I do not know whether these conditions can be said to hold in respect of the TRC. The force of the victims' complaints is that they do not. But if they do then there seems no reason to suppose that some other value has been traded for justice. All that has happened is that different interests have reached a just accommodation, an outcome for which there is no abstract measure.

The foregoing considerations bring us to our second issue: can the purposes of the TRC be construed as encompassing those of ordinary criminal and civil justice? The compromise approach argues that retributive goals are not wholly lost sight of in the pursuit of reconciliation. But this seems questionable, even if the character of the retribution supposedly involved is not so qualified as to fall before the charge of injustice. For what are these retributive goals? The TRC's Final Report claims that what is obtained are an admission of a responsibility by the perpetrator, and exposure to public shaming and its effects. Some have likened the process to the perpetrator's confession in plea bargaining.[41] By his confession the perpetrator makes an acknowledgement of wrong-doing, which it is the first aim of punishment to achieve.

Whatever the merits of such a dilute retributivism, its application here seems wide of the mark. In the first place the perpetrator's admission of responsibility is not a confession in the relevant sense: it is simply an acknowledgement that an act *in fact* wrong was performed; it is not so far an acknowledgement that the act *was* wrong. Thus if an aim of retribution is to secure repentance, then appearance before the TRC does not take even the first step towards that. Secondly, if shaming occurs – and this will surely depend upon the company the perpetrator keeps – this is entirely incidental and no necessary part of the message the TRC proceedings send. If retribution aims to convey a message of defeat to the criminal from the court, here he can walk away still victorious.

The advantage of a restorative justice approach is that it can recognise that such retributive goals are *not* served by the TRC, and still insist that justice *is*; and, what is more, the justice which is part and parcel of the ordinary administration of criminal and civil law. The model of restorative justice involved here is that of justice as conflict resolution rather than reparation. The TRC certainly *took* restorative justice in this sense to be its task – the task of establishing the truth and thereby effecting, as one proponent of the restorative conception expresses it, 'the restoration into safe communities of victims and offenders who have resolved their conflicts'.[42] Is this a plausible way to view the TRC's operations as effecting the delivery of justice?

It would only be so, I suggest, if we view it not as a psychological but as an essentially symbolic process, and, what is more, one where the parties are not just individual victims and perpetrators, but black South Africans and the beneficiaries of apartheid with whom they must make peace. This requires a moral restoration of communal relations, which depends precisely upon establishing equal respect, and thereby, it may be claimed, delivering justice.

I move now, then, to considering how the transition to such relationships which the TRC seeks to facilitate affects the question of how it can deliver justice. The first thing to note, it seems to me, is that although the collapse of apartheid was negotiated and the ANC had suspended its military campaign, nonetheless the regime had suffered a defeat in what was a low-level civil war. It is for this reason that one of the principal aims of punishment simply cannot be served in the present context, namely the prevention of further crimes by past offenders. Those who tortured and killed for the regime are no longer in a position to do so; those who engaged in anti-state terrorist actions no longer have a motive. The special treatment reserved to political crimes by the TRC is a tacit acknowledgement of facts like these. Whatever form of justice is appropriate to handling the transition must equally take account of the nature of the shift in power that is involved here.

It is, I suggest, not a question of how a principled compromise between retribution and stability can be reached that is crucial, but rather of how, at the conclusion of a conflict, two sides with different conceptions of community and different values can be brought together in social equality and concord. This will happen only if the transition is handled justly, and this means, in this context, where the perpetrators of crimes connected with the conflict are treated justly. The retribution that critics of the TRC demanded would, arguably, not have been just. It would have been perceived as 'victor's justice', a form of revenge lacking a moral point discernible to the perpetrator who sees himself as occupying a community other than that of the avenger.[43] It would also have stood in the way of integrating him into a single multi-racial community, which was the TRC's aim, not just at the personal, but at the symbolic level.

The perpetration of rights abuses by those who operated the apartheid system demonstrated their repudiation of a principle of equal respect, a repudiation grounded in convictions, however odious. By declining to subject the perpetrators to a judgement based on an application of the principle of equal respect, which they flouted, the TRC achieves two things. First, it escapes any charge of imposing values not accepted by the perpetrator and hence impotent to influence him. Second, it thereby accords him equal respect as an autonomous agent, able to choose from what principles to act (though this does not, of course, imply any respect for his principles). This practical operation of the principle of equal respect exemplifies the justice which, it is hoped, will form the 'bond', in Cicero's phrase,[44] of a single political community – a community within which gross human rights violations will not be possible from the sorts of principles that licence them under apartheid.

It is creating this 'bond of justice' that is, I suggest, the goal of the TRC. Crucial to it is equal treatment for like actions. And this is where, it seems to me, it is important that ANC freedom fighters were equally arraigned before the TRC as the state terrorists of the apartheid regime. It would, of course, have been unthinkable that ANC fighters should have been punished for attacks which occurred in what they took to be a just war. Arguably the security forces of apartheid were on morally weaker ground, breaking laws which they officially enforced. But to treat them both alike and punish neither, only on condition that a trial of the facts, so to speak, was made, was an object lesson in the transition to an order in which equal treatment would prevail as a principle of justice.

Notes

1. See Chris Brown, 'Humanitarian Intervention and International Political Theory', in A. Moseley & R. Norman (eds), *Human Rights and Military Intervention* (Aldershot: Ashgate, 2002).
2. Article 2 (4).
3. Michael Walzer's concept: *Just and Unjust Wars* (New York: Basic, 1977), ch. 4.
4. For the liberal conception, see e.g. Will Kymlicka, *Liberalism, Community and Culture* (Oxford: Oxford University Press, 1989); for the communitarian, Michael Walzer, *Just and Unjust Wars*.

5. Cosmopolitanism can, in fact, take a variety of forms. See Nigel Dower, *World Ethics: the New Agenda* (Edinburgh: Edinburgh University Press, 1988).

6. Cp. Nigel Dower, *World Ethics*, p. 19.

7. E.g. Costas Douzinas, *The End of Human Rights* (Oxford: Hart, 2000), chs 5 and 6.

8. Hedley Bull, *The Anarchical Society* (Houndmills: Macmillan, 1977), p. 317.

9. Geoffrey Robertson, *Crimes against Humanity* (Harmondsworth: Penguin, 2000), pp. 403–11.

10. Statutes of International Court of Justice Art. 38, cited D.W. Greig, *International Law* (London: Butterworths, 1970), p. 6.

11. Christine Gray, *International Law and the Use of Force* (Oxford: Oxford University Press, 2000), pp. 41–2.

12. Antonio Tanca, *Foreign Armed Intervention in Internal Conflict* (Dordrecht: Martinus Nijhoff, 1993), p. 114.

13. For a discussion of the concept of repression see my *Terrorism, Security and Nationality* (London: Routledge, 1994), pp. 156 f.

14. See A.C. Arend & R.J. Beck, *International Law and the Use of Force* (London: Routledge, 1993), ch. 8.

15. *Second Treatise on Civil Government* (many editions, 1690), sect. 226.

16. Cp. Georg Hegel *Philosophy of Right*, sect. 349, quoted and discussed by Mervyn Frost, *Ethics in International Relations* (Cambridge: Cambridge University Press, 1996), p. 152.

17. I do not discuss the issue here. Suffice to say that some such interventions can seem imperialistic, for few would wish to follow J.S. Mill in defending intervention amongst 'barbarous people', 'A Few Words on Non-Intervention', *Collected Works*, vol. XXI (Toronto: Toronto University Press, 1984), pp. 111–24.

18. However, international law does recognise that in a situation of 'belligerency' the state really has lost authority in that part of its territory over which rebels have taken control, so that it is now up to them to exercise jurisdiction there, pending possible recapture by state forces. See A.V.W. & A.J. Thomas, *Non-Intervention* (Dallas: Southern Methodist Press, 1956), pp. 215–21.

19. 'Qualified sovereigntism' as Charles Jones calls it: *Global Justice* (Oxford: Oxford University Press, 1999), p. 214.

20. See above p. 35. In the circumstances described this would exemplify what Allen Buchanan calls a 'remedial' right of secession. *Secession* (Boulder: Westview, 1991), pp. 27–81.

21. So Richard Norman's objection to Michael Walzer's justification for defensive war does not apply here, since it is the lives of the minority, not some abstract political community that is being defended. See Norman, *Ethics, Killing and War* (Cambridge: Cambridge University Press, 1995), pp. 132–9.

22. Nor are these just war principles idle. For if military action is undertaken on behalf of a group of people then they must have some control

over it, which the terms of an alliance provide. 'One cannot,' as Walzer puts it, 'intervene on their behalf and against their ends': *Just and Unjust Wars*, p. 104. But this is a demand for which the cosmopolitan conception has no place.

23. Cp. Antonio Tanca, *Foreign Armed Intervention*, pp. 76–81.
24. See Christine Gray, *International Law*, pp. 115–19.
25. Derived from the 'millet' system: see Ralph Grillo, *Pluralism and the Politics of Difference* (Oxford: Oxford University Press, 1998), ch. 4.
26. Cp. Geoffrey Robertson, *Crimes against Humanity*, pp. 315 f., 335 f.
27. Cp. Peter A. French, 'Unchosen Evil and Moral Responsibility', in A. Jokić (ed.), *War Crimes and Collective Wrongdoing* (Malden, MA: Blackwell, 2001), p. 39.
28. *Pace* Alan Gewirth, 'War Crimes and Human Rights' in ibid., p. 51.
29. See Burleigh T. Wilkins, 'Whose Trials? – Whose Reconciliations?' in ibid., p. 95.
30. Quoted Robert Alexy, 'A Defence of Radbruch's Formula', in D. Dyzenhaus (ed.), *Recrafting the Rule of Law* (Oxford: Hart, 1999), p. 16.
31. E.g. Geoffrey Robertson, *Crimes against Humanity*, pp. 256 f.
32. See C.J. Arnson (ed.), *Comparative Peace Processes in Latin America* (Washington, DC: Woodrow Wilson Center, 1999).
33. *The Irish Times*, 13 January, 2000.
34. J. Allen, 'Balancing Justice and Social Unity', *University of Toronto Law Journal* 49(1999).
35. J.J. Llewellyn & R. House, 'Institutions for Restorative Justice' in ibid.
36. See David A. Crocker, 'Transitional Justice and International Civil Society', in Jokić (ed.), *War Crimes*.
37. Quoted Llewellyn & House, 'Institutions for Restorative Justice', p. 369.
38. Quoted Ted Honderich, *Punishment* (Harmondsworth: Penguin), p. 22.
39. Quoted Thomas Baldwin, 'Punishment, Communication and Resentment', in M. Matravers (ed.), *Punishment and Political Theory* (Oxford: Hart, 1999), p. 129.
40. See Ted Honderich, *Punishment*, ch. 2 for discussion.
41. E.g. Dan Markel, 'The Justice of Amnesty? Towards a Theory of Retributivism in Recovering States', *University of Toronto Law Journal* 49(1999), p. 437.
42. Daniel Van Ness quoted A. von Hirsch & A. Ashworth (eds.), *Principled Sentencing* (Oxford: Hart, 1998), p. 301.
43. Cp. Alan Norrie, 'Albert Speer And "The Space Between"', in M. Matravers (ed.), *Punishment and Political Theory*, p. 136.
44. Cicero, *De republica* (many translations) III 31.

7

Restoring Peace

Ending new wars

The eruption of new wars raises three urgent questions: how to end them; how to resolve the conflicts that give rise to them; and how to produce the conditions in which they are unlikely to occur. The contribution of a philosopher to answering such questions is inevitably limited – limited only, perhaps, to identifying and scrutinising the assumptions involved in some of the answers. Yet the questions are practical ones, and, as such, they have not only a pragmatic but an ethical aspect. In the theory of the just war the aim of war ought to be a just peace. But it is crucial to realise that a just peace is not to be understood as peace plus justice. In distinguishing between defensive and punitive versions of just war theory I was at pains to point out that whereas on the former conception the proper aim of war is peace and security it is only on the latter that it is justice. So on the defensive version which I am commending the aim of a just peace should not be understood to be a peace which delivers justice, desirable as this may be. Rather justice should be taken to characterise the peace obtained, not to be an element additional to it. What makes a peace just, then, rather than unjust is that it does not impose unreasonable terms on the vanquished as a result of victory. That is to say, victory must not be exploited for ends other than those of establishing peace with a fair degree of security, for to do so would be tantamount to turning a defensive war into an aggressive one in which political advantages over and above security were achieved by war. With this in mind we can ask: How are new wars to be ended justly? What sort of a secure peace should follow them? And, most ambitiously, what would a world order be like in which the risk of wars mounted by sub-state actors is, at least, minimised?

We start, then, with ending particular new wars, and here there are, as with all wars, two possible kinds of ending: military or diplomatic. Wars are ended either by the victory of one side, which is able to impose its will upon the other; or by a negotiated peace, sometimes as a result of military stalemate, at others to avert a total defeat. There is, however, immense resistance on the part of states to negotiate with sub-state opponents, who are branded as terrorists partly to justify such reluctance.[1] Several related considerations might be mustered to support this attitude. One is that members of militant sub-state groups are merely criminals, and the proper response is to catch and punish, not to negotiate with them. For to negotiate will grant them a spurious standing, which cannot be obtained by criminal acts of violence. So far this argument scarcely advances matters, since it simply reflects the state's attitude towards its opponents as people engaging in private acts of intimidation, rather than public and properly political acts of war. The argument does not justify the attitude, and we have, at the end of the last chapter, cast doubt on its presumption that crime, in such a context, should always be punished anyway. Two other considerations might be adduced to strengthen the argument. The first is the consequentialist idea that terrorists should not be rewarded, by allowing them to 'bomb their way to the negotiating table' (or, indeed, to effect any change of policy by such means), since this will increase the incidence of terror. Like all such calculations, the conclusion of this one is at best uncertain, especially if, as is likely, no promising non-violent avenues are open to sub-state groups. If actual experience is consulted, as in such calculations it should be, the moral seems to be that terrorism continues so long as no negotiations are offered.

The dogma that they should not be depends upon a rather different development of the argument, namely that sub-state violence breaches the conventions required for negotiation, so that terrorists cannot be admitted to them as parties in good standing. This, however, seems fanciful. The threat of renewed or escalating violence on both sides is an undercurrent of all negotiations involved in the ending of wars. To suppose that it disenfranchises sub-state groups from talks may again reflect a reluctance to admit that war is in fact what is occurring. If it is specifically the kind of unlawful violence to which they commonly resort that disqualifies them then it has to be said that in such conflicts the state itself is seldom blameless in its methods, and, even if it is, it should seek to bring its opponents into line with the law. While they remain beyond the pale as parties to negotiation, sub-state groups have little motive for abiding by the rules that constrain such actors in their political roles. Once they are included they need not only to exercise their power but to justify its exercise to others, and this gives them a motive, even though not always a sufficient one, for showing restraint. The aim of negotiation, then, in the case of new wars, should be not only to end them, but to reintegrate their participants into a political society – international or domestic – from which their deviation from its rules has detached them.

This is not, of course, to say that they must renounce violence altogether to be admitted. That is both unrealistic and partial, since established states will not themselves ever make such renunciations. Nor is it conducive to a clear sighted appreciation of the situation. The fact of violence, even of unlawful violence, is an important constituent of the situation, indicative of the strength of feelings involved in a people's cause and the degree of animosity towards some other people characterised in terms of their identity. But while these feelings animate the parties in conflict they can be held in abeyance, as it were, in negotiation, since its participants share a common political role which requires mutual respect and an effort at understanding. It is these attitudes, it must be hoped, which will be transmitted from political leaders to their followers, so that the inflamed interactions of identity groups are replaced by normal politics. No doubt many factors will stand in the way of this. What should be avoided, however, are attitudes which deny opponents an exit from violence with honour and which motivate the very sentiments of resentment and revenge which, as we have seen, are at the root of many of the horrors of new wars.

The aim of negotiation to end a conflict is to determine what can be accepted as a just peace that provides both sides with security. What counts as reasonable here, given the power relations between the parties, is something which can be established only by the practice of statesmen, acting within their roles and responding to the demands upon them both as representatives of groups and as members of international society. The intention must be to import such standards into negotiations designed to end new wars as well. Security for both sides here will, as in old wars, require political differences to be addressed, for peace, it is often remarked,[2] is not a mere cessation of hostilities; it requires a resolution of the conflicts that led to them sufficient to provide no reason for their return.

How might the kind of conflict which produced new wars be resolved? At first sight it seems obvious that the conflict should be resolved justly; yet what is to count as bringing about a just settlement of identity conflict is far from clear. What lie at the heart of new wars, I have suggested, are conflicts over which collective identities are to be recognised politically in some particular way. Yet, I have claimed, such questions about political legitimacy are, in themselves, not questions of justice at all. There are *no* good cases for claiming that some set of political arrangements would be legitimate with respect to some identity group and hence no injustice is done them by denying it to them. It follows that if this is all that the conflict underlying some new war concerns then there is no such thing as the outcome of a settlement that is just, as against a settlement that is so perceived by one side or another, or even by both. There is, though, the question of whether the *manner* of settling the conflict is just, and also of whether, insofar as it concerns other issues than legitimacy, its outcome is just; we shall consider these questions before returning to the central and most difficult one.

Conflicts can be resolved in two ways: by a settlement determined upon by an impartial adjudicator, or by a negotiation between the parties. Much conflict resolution involves elements of each, but they do have different features. The former, 'external' settlement, as we may call it, depends upon an analysis of the reasons for conflict and the production of a plan which either eliminates them or addresses them sufficiently to prevent further war and which is imposed upon the parties. This is typically the kind of settlement involved, at least as an interim measure, when external intervention has deprived a territory of effective governance, as in Kosovo. An external settlement can itself be of two types. It can be purely pragmatic, seeking to identify and correct underlying causes of conflict, such as lack of economic opportunity for one group, or to manage its symptoms, for example by segregating people. It can, on the other hand, be, as it were, juridical, looking at grievances and weighing them against some standard of justice, and only such a process can be thought of as aiming at a just method of settlement.

It is evident, as I have just hinted, that when an external settlement is juridical it may fail to commend itself to the parties in conflict because the standards of justice it rests upon are not theirs. What counts as treating people fairly, however, differs in different societies, depending upon a host of understandings that some people take for granted and that others reject, understandings that are themselves consequent upon differences in people's social practices. It is just such divergent understandings that distinguish, for example, the settler's opinion that he has a just claim to land which he has brought under cultivation and the native's view that she is thereby unjustly deprived of its use, even though she had no claim to property in it. And from such disagreements large political conflicts, erupting into violence, can emerge, as over land use in parts of Indonesia and South America, for instance. If these conflicts are to be resolved then the settlement reached must be an 'internal' one, in the sense of being negotiated between the parties, rather than imposed from without. For whatever the effectiveness of an external settlement might be, it could not be regarded as one reached fairly, through taking account of the parties' own standards of what is just.

The conclusion is, I believe, a quite general one: for a settlement to be arrived at justly it must be one that the parties could in principle recognise as just in the circumstances in accordance with their own standards, and for that to be the case it must be a settlement they make between themselves.[3] This is a result particularly pertinent to the conflicts of identity politics. For many – perhaps all – of these conflicts involve divergences in what ends of action are valued. A resolution requires a grasp by both sides of each others' values. How, though, with different values, is a resolution even possible? We need to distinguish two sorts of process here. The first is straightforward enough. It is a mere acknowledgement that something is valued to a certain extent by an opponent who is prepared to fight for it – a territory of virgin forest, say, like the West Irian province of Indonesia. Conceding it, however, would involve relinquishing something valued by one's own lights, for example an opportunity for economic development. One kind of resolution involves an attempt to compromise upon what are perceived as competing interests, so that each side gets some of what they want but not all. Such a compromise may or may not be possible, but whether it is just depends upon the degree to which it does take account of each side's values, rather than only the strength of their bargaining position. Neither side will think it has got what is its just due, but the compromise may still be recognised as a just one. Compromises of this sort are the stuff of politics and it is a mark of statesmanship to be able to negotiate an equitable compromise, in this sense, without either abusing power or moralistically neglecting interests, for it is within political society oriented towards peace that equity of this sort is recognised.

The second sort of process requires not just a grasp of the fact that something is valued but an understanding of why it is and thus, to this extent an imaginative grasp of the opponent's motivation. The aim of such a process is not compromise but reconciliation,[4] in which that some end is valued by an opponent is not just accepted as a fact about her, but is acknowledged as something which, within her own way of life, is to be supported rather than deplored. A settlement made on this basis will aim to facilitate the pursuit of her ends as much as possible, and not merely to tolerate them. A settlement resulting from such a process may, in principle, be accepted by both sides as producing a just outcome, since each will have done its best to promote the other's ends by her own lights and in accordance with her own standards. That neither's values determines the outcome exclusively can be recognised by both sides as fair, rather than as a deviation from justice. For if it is regarded as a deviation then this is indicative of a failure to achieve reconciliation. What must be stressed, however, is that reconciliation in the sense intended here does *not* imply that people can necessarily continue to live peaceably within the polity. The reconciliation is effected between their leaders who may grant that, while each side's ends are worthwhile, their pursuit within the same polity is impossible, so that a reconciliatory settlement is as compatible with partition for example, as it is with mutual accommodation within a shared state.[5]

I have assumed that the sorts of issue needing to be resolved by compromise or reconciliation are those, like occupation of territory, that are not directly concerned with questions of legitimacy, but rather with questions where a just outcome can uncontroversially be sought. I return to competing legitimacy claims which do not, I have argued, admit of such an outcome. What they do admit of, however, are settlements whose process is a just one; and again, I would claim, this rules out external settlements which are likely to be skewed by the arbitrator's own conception of legitimacy – a German ethnically based one, for example, delivers a different verdict on whether Kosovo should become an independent state from an American multiculturalist one. Internal negotiation of a compromise may be one kind of just process in some political circumstances. Where, for example, an ethnic criterion of political identity is adopted by one group but rejected by the state in which it finds itself, then regional autonomy for the group is an obvious case of a compromise between the group's separatist demands and the state's insistence on its legitimacy by some non-ethnic criterion. But, without appreciation on both sides of the other's valuation of one kind of collectivity as a focus for particular attachments rather than another, it is likely to be unstable. Kosovo again provides an example, where regional autonomy was diluted by the Yugoslav government, partly as a result of increasing ethnic identification by Albanians – a move that proved so tragically counter-productive that a long term return to this arrangement may no longer prove possible.

How, though, can the reconciliatory process sketched above be applied to disputes about legitimacy? What the parties will need to grasp is how associating together in the different ways they do can realise values that play a worthwhile part in their respective ways of life. This may be more or less easy, depending upon the degree of divergence of the forms of association and the extent to which they claim the exclusive loyalties of their members. Thus in a world of post-Westphalian states, Western societies have found it particularly hard to comprehend the prioritising of Islam as a focus of obligation and allegiance in some parts of the East. It has been easier to appreciate attachment to small cultural communities based on a minority language, even though it is not one that provides a ready access to a modernising culture; for most Western states are founded upon a common language. In any particular set of circumstances there may or may not be a way of integrating the pursuit of such different ends of association within a single state, and whether there is will partly depend upon the preparedness of its people generally to appreciate each other's differences and even celebrate them.

In any case, however, a reconciliatory settlement is something that can only be worked out and decided upon by those involved.

Whether the outcome is just will obviously not depend upon whether some criterion of legitimacy has been rightly applied or not, since *ex hypothesi* there is no agreed criterion, and, if I am right, no criterion recommendable by reason. The outcome will not be just, then, because it issues in legitimate political arrangements. It will be just because it takes account, to the fullest extent possible, of the ends of association which the parties in conflict believe to justify their legitimacy claims, and this is something that only those with a feeling for those ends can adjudicate upon.

Preventing war

It follows from the foregoing remarks about conflict resolution that there are no general solutions to the sorts of problems that give rise to new wars; still less, solutions that are available *a priori*. In considering how fresh wars can be prevented, however, we need to look at the features of states and the characteristics of identity groups which together militate against peace, and ask how they might change in ways conducive to it. With respect to states there are, broadly speaking, two prevailing schools of thought. One, which we have met with already, is cosmopolitanism. It views the underlying problem as one of injustice which arises from the capacity of states to violate the human rights of their own citizens with impunity and to ignore the claims of the citizens of other states, for example, to a fair share of the world's wealth. Thus minorities within states can be oppressed and conditions created in other states that conduce to sectional oppression as a result of scarcity of resources. The solution is greatly to reduce the powers of states, for example by allowing humanitarian intervention on the one hand and requiring redistribution of resources on the other. We have already had cause to criticise the former suggestion. And an adequate treatment of the latter would take us too far away from our theme.[6]

The general problem with cosmopolitanism is that it postulates a supposedly ideal state of things without giving any coherent account of how this is to be reached from where we are. Nor is this a merely pragmatic problem. Since cosmopolitanism tends to neglect the fact that political values are acquired within particular cultural frameworks it supposes that assent to its principles of greater global jurisdiction and control is resisted principally because of sectional self-interest,[7] rather than because of an attachment to political arrangements that are well enough understood to be operated within, however adversarially. There is no reason for cosmopolitan optimism that greater transnational contacts will dispel such attitudes. For, insofar as they exist, transnational contacts are typically made within the existing state system, where what unites states is precisely that very political independence and territorial control which cosmopolitans seek to qualify. It is, furthermore, *as* citizens of states that we appreciate the extent to which they act justly or unjustly. Cosmopolitanism provides no convincing alternative account of how such judgements might be shareable across cultural boundaries.

The second prevailing view about how states should change in order to promote peace is nationalism or some other related version of the politics of identity itself. The diagnosis here is that states take insufficient account of national identities. 'The state as a purely institutional entity has no natural boundaries,' the argument runs, 'and a system composed of such units is likely to be conflict-prone and power-oriented.'[8] The extreme nationalist prescription, then, is a greater correspondence between states and nations, while somewhat more moderate positions countenance federalism, consociationalism or other arrangements in which the basic political unit is the identity group. The rationale for this may be that such groups are people's natural foci of allegiance or that they are their chosen ones. In any event, the proximate causes of violence will be removed by building states around them rather than trying to suppress them. But here we already see the insuperable problem with the nationalist account, which, we have previously noticed, is that there is no agreed criterion of what kind of group should count as a nation and thus of what should provide a state with its 'natural boundaries'. People do not agree on whether this is a matter to be decided by certain objective facts about them – ethnicity, history or whatever – or by the sentiments of attachment they feel. If it is the former, the complex facts about people's groupings and sub-groupings do not, in any case, yield a system of disjoint groups to which a system of states could correspond. If the latter, then again, since people's sentiments are not simple or stable they yield no suitable system of groups to underpin a system of states. Whatever system is set in place cleavages of identity are likely to emerge so long as they can be exploited for political ends.[9]

The trouble with the state system is, one might argue, from the standpoint of a politics of role, exactly the opposite of that which nationalism diagnoses. The system is matched *too* closely to groups which can, by some criterion or other – the choice being based on considerations of political expediency – be counted as nations. And the match is demanded as a result of the myth of legitimacy, which insists on some relationship between state and people which transforms it from 'a purely institutional entity' to one whose boundaries are somehow justified, not merely in terms of what may be needed in particular political circumstances, but in accordance with some systematic principles for dividing the world into states. None, I have argued, is available, and recognition of this fact should go some way to unmasking many of the claims that lead to conflict. A world in which states were acknowledged to be 'purely institutional' would be, to that extent at least, a safer world, for whatever conflicts within it there were would be conflicts of interests, and there is no reason to think that these are somehow decreased by subscription to the myth of legitimacy. Indeed, there is every reason to think that identity struggles are commonly rooted in conflicts of interest. Yet, while this may often explain their origins, identity groups can persist long after changes in patterns of interest are made irrelevant, and they can draw in people entirely unaffected by interest concerns, perpetuating and widening conflict.[10]

Cosmopolitanism, however, shares with nationalism the assumptions underlying what I have called the myth of legitimacy, namely, that unless people have special obligations to fellow members of some group then there is no justification for having state boundaries drawn around any group. In sharp contrast to nationalists, they deny that there *are* any such special obligations, and hence go on to attack the state system in its present form as an institution enforcing such obligations. But rejecting the myth of legitimacy allows special obligations to derive simply from membership of a well constituted and properly functioning state. They have – and need – no further grounding than the fact that they are required of people in their role as citizens of such states. The moral to draw, then, may be that so long as the obligations expected of people go as far as and not beyond what citizenship requires, and are owed to others only as citizens, then there is, so far, no good reason for purely political conflict within the state; that what causes such conflict is either the imposition of unwanted obligations or the exclusion of some people from benefiting from their performance.

Laying aside the myth of a legitimacy grounded in shared nationality implies that the state has no reason to create a strong community, in the sense of one pursuing a common good rooted in shared ethical ends beyond those implicit in citizenship itself. These more limited ends, we may suggest, are simply those of peace and harmony in the co-operative pursuit of common interests under a system of law. The common interests involved are those that derive from occupancy of a shared space, which does not yet imply shared ethical ends, though divergent values can, of course, lead to conflicts of interest. What are to count as common interests which the state is to assist in pursuing will vary from state to state, depending upon what areas of co-operation or competition actually exist among its people. But what a state that rightly abjures the creation of a strong community should resist is the identification of common interests through the designation of an ethical end as shared by citizens because it is – or is supposed to be – an aspect of their shared national (or analogous) identity. And a state should resist this precisely because it would be expecting of some citizens more than their own values may lead them to offer, and stigmatising those who do not offer more as failing to deserve the reciprocal benefits of fellow citizenship.[11]

This brings us, then, from the question of what sort of feature of state practice may be modified in order to remove some common causes of new wars to that of how identity groups might change. If states do play down their supposed national character without losing their status as the loci of specifically political special obligations, then, correspondingly, identity groups should, I have suggested, possess less reason to demand a separate political existence. They will not be able to claim, on the one hand, that they are discriminated against because the ethical ends promoted by the state are not their own, nor, on the other, that they are oppressed – or worse – for failing to conform. If they demand a polity in which their ends specifically are promoted then they are going beyond what it is reasonable to expect of it, since this will require of citizens a commitment beyond the requirements of their role. There is a sense, then, in which, in a politics of role, citizenship between states is interchangeable: the essential requirements are the same, though in practice how they are understood will depend upon the particular cultures of a state's members and its political history of their rights and duties. Thus it should not be thought that the politics of role sketched here is simply a version of the liberalism which developed in Western states after the Reformation. For this is a particular historical and social phenomenon, with arguably, a commitment to the value of freedom, understood in a way beyond what is necessary merely for harmonious citizenship.

What is crucial to the account offered by a politics of role is that citizenship of a given state should be viewed as, in a sense, an accident, dependent upon no relation between the identity of the citizen and the character of the state. The common good that such citizens aim at – the harmonious pursuit of shared interests – is aimed at simply because it is the good of the citizens of the state in which one finds oneself. It is not aimed at because of any prior evaluation of the ends that such and such a people pursue. It is therefore entirely different from the good of a national community, which consists in the pursuit of some ethical end picked out in terms of the essential features of its members' national identity. Thus nationalists do not promote the good of their fellow citizens just because they are fellow citizens. They promote it because they are, say, speakers of the same language or adherents of the same faith. They set a value on a community constituted by sharing that language or that faith, so that those who attach no special value to these kinds of relationship or the sorts of cultural flourishing they promote will be effectively excluded from the national community. The designation of such ethical ends, moreover, is what allows more to be demanded of members of a group than simple citizenship requires of them.

It is this, I am suggesting, that is a potent cause of wars. For it may, on the one hand, demand from group members support for political separation for their nation, rather than mere self-defence by an oppressed people through the creation of a new polity in which they can enjoy the benefits of equal citizenship. On the other hand, it may demand of all citizens of a state that they think of themselves as joined in a wider project than a peaceful life in common. This may not only have the effect, as already indicated, of alienating those who do not value it, creating unrest and fomenting secession – even secession justified by their subsequent oppression. It may also lead to irredentist and related movements, where the project in common is seen to be shared with others outside the state. Examples include the bringing together of speakers of the same language, as in moves to unite Kosovo with Albania, or of co-religionists, as with Pan-Islamism – all of which destabilise borders and cause conflicts. A sceptical view of cosmopolitanism will regard it in a similar light, as seeking to break down the boundaries against a general imposition of what are, in fact, Western values.

It seems plausible to locate the roots of identity struggles in conflicts of interest. Yet these conflicts are typically unequal. On one side are the relatively powerless and oppressed, whose harnessing of the politics of identity to their cause may be an understandable gambit in the defence of a group, however incalculable its consequences. On the other, however, are already powerful states, whose motive for mobilising interest groups behind shared values is the extension of their capacity to control world events in their own interests at the expense of those of others. What the norms of international society aim to put in place are checks upon such ventures, in the form, especially, of rules restricting resort to war and its conduct. Statesmen, through changing epochs in the balance of power, have seen such restraints as generally serving the purposes of states in achieving peaceable common lives for their citizens, and citizens have thus seen them as in their interests *as* citizens. They do not, in themselves, prevent wars, nor the power struggles that wars express. Yet they do partially succeed in exposing wars for what they are and in appealing to shareable standards for judging them as justified or unjustified, fought honourably or otherwise. A politics of role seeks, in the interests of peace, to preserve such a system against erosion by ethical projects that are, on the one hand, too partial or, on the other, too ambitious in their scope. But whether it can do so in any particular pattern of power relations is a practical, not a theoretical question.

A return to roles

Cosmopolitanism is right to reject a politics of identity in which states aim to create what I have called 'strong communities' with distinctive ethical ends shared by their members. But it is wrong, I claim, to do so because it detects overarching ends shareable not just by members of particular identity groups but by human beings per se. In this respect cosmopolitanism is insufficiently unlike identity politics. It too locates the source of what we ought to do in who we are, rather than, as with the politics of role, in what we are. And it too does so by attempting to locate certain values which – now as human beings alone – we can recognise and seek to realise. What is presupposed is that there is a good for man which can be attained by the realisation of such values, among others, and that the good man or woman is one who realises them.

The politics of role makes no such assumption. It supposes only that in our lives we perform a multiplicity of roles, each with its own standards of performance, for maintaining which we are responsible to those to whom the role relates us. No overall conception of what is good is involved in this, only of what is good in respect of particular roles. What it is to be a good man or woman over and above performing well the roles in which one finds oneself is a question not answered within the ethical framework of the politics of role. But for all that the framework *is* ethical. Not all functions are such that performing them well does contribute to a good life, for the standards that regulate role performance are not just those of technical efficiency, but of compliance with social expectation. Indeed it is through interaction with those to whom the role relates us that these standards are hammered out. There is a sense, then, in which the ethics that the politics of role presupposes is grounded in professional ethics – that is to say the ethics of particular professions, though not of course only of professions – rather than professional ethics being somehow shaped by overarching ethical values. And as our different roles require different virtues – courage and chivalry for a soldier, say; gentleness and concern for a parent – so this ethical framework leaves room for a plurality of values, without any necessary prioritisation of some over others as contributory to a good life.

The politics of role, I suggested at the outset, is an essentially classical conception of how people participate in politics. It derives from Greek models of citizenship and comes to fruition in Roman notions of this status as available quite independently of group identity. Thus Cicero, in his *De republica*, defines a political community as 'an association united by a common sense of right and a community of interest',[12] where that common sense of right is manifest in acceptance of a shared system of justice which brings order to their social life, and the community of interest derives from the need to get along together in the same territory. Acting in conformity with this conception is what is required of citizens. Justice, Cicero maintains, is 'much the most glorious and splendid of all the virtues',[13] but he treats it as a virtue displayed principally in our public role as fellow citizens with others. It is also exhibited, however, in the right conduct of war, where 'there are certain peculiar laws of war…which are of all things most strictly to be observed' by one who takes on a military role – a decision, Cicero stresses, which must only be made for the right reason, namely the service of the state.[14,15]

While Cicero's practical conception of duties roots them, for the most part, firmly in the performance of roles, his idea of their origin in human reason derives from a cosmopolitanism owed to Stoic influences and always attractive to imperialists, Roman or otherwise. It is, however, a detachable and better detached, feature of his account. Much later when Machiavelli implicitly criticises Cicero in *The Prince* it is this feature that he attacks, denying that there is any independent source in morality for the *virtú* of a ruler.[16] Yet Machiavelli, in failing to distinguish the ethical from the purely technical requirements of a role, is forced to accept a view of morality as independent of role performance and hence to contrast it, just like any cosmopolitan, with the practice of politics in advancing the interests of the state. That said, it is clear that a classical conception of the politics of role as furnishing ethical standards formed an important tradition in Western thinking, to be drawn upon across the centuries when conditions required it.

We may conveniently trace the intrusion of the politics of identity to St Augustine's critique of Cicero's account of political community. Instead of the community of interests and shared system of justice that Cicero discerns in the Roman republic, Augustine is struck by its cultural diversity: 'All the similarity of their human nature is of no avail to unite them in fellowship. So true is this that a man would be more cheerful with his dog for company than with a foreigner.'[17] For, Augustine thinks 'that commonwealth never existed because there never was real justice in the community'.[18] Real justice is to be found only among a community of Christian believers, for 'justice is found where God, the one supreme God rules an obedient City according to his grace.'[19] Thus Augustine denies that there can be anything which counts as a system of justice whereby a community's affairs could be regulated irrespective of its members' religious or other cultural attachments. Yet peoples or communities in *some* sense can be distinguished, so that even the Roman state 'certainly was a commonwealth to some degree, according to more plausible definitions' than that of Cicero.[20] The 'more plausible definition' that Augustine offers, as we saw earlier, is that 'a people is the association of a multitude of rational beings united by a common agreement on the objects of their love.'[21] Here is a clear expression of the politics of identity: people enter the political realm already differentiated by their moral values, in ways that politics may accommodate but can never overcome.

The identity politics of religious affiliation led in modern times, I have suggested, to the Thirty Years' War with all its horrors. The Treaty of Westphalia and the modern state system it instituted represented a return to more classical models of political involvement and, in consequence, of war as to be fought in defence of a state's interest and not for any wider religious or moral purposes. We have, in short, a return to the politics of role, as a reaction to and defence against the destructive effects of an untrammelled politics of identity.

The Westphalian system makes possible a code of international relations between states which transforms them, in Hedley Bull's terms, from a mere system into a society.[22] Such a society, he maintains, is geared to preserve the system of states, their independence and sovereignty, peace between them and those goals of social life which consist in the security of persons and their possessions and the keeping of promises and agreements – goals that states themselves seek to achieve. The way in which these aims are realised is by putting in place a panoply of customary rules and formal regulations governing relations between states and, to some degree, conduct within them. While this constitutes a body of international law which is addressed principally to states, it is the behaviour of statesmen which is, in fact, constrained by requirements which determine the content of their international role. What is made possible is a form of relationship between people which enables them to meet and negotiate on matters which affect the interests of the states they represent. Without rules that are generally honoured such meetings would be impossible. Those that are hammered out over time by mutual agreement are what give international society its particular form and hence shape the role of statesmen within it.

In recent times the United Nations' Charter and the various formal pronouncements of the Organisation have codified many of the rules that give content to the statesman's role. One relatively minor example may illustrate the way in which this role prescinds from one dimension of identity. The UN Convention on the Elimination of Racial Discrimination affirms that 'discrimination between human beings on the grounds of race, colour or ethnic origin is an obstacle to friendly and peaceful relations among nations.'[23] What is clearly assumed is that different states will be occupied by different ethnic groups, so that, in international society, their leaders will have to deal with members of groups other than their own. These sorts of relationship will be impossible if these leaders take up racist attitudes to one another. They will be unable to confer on the friendly terms required for international society if they treat each other with aversion and contempt. However, it is not only the personal attitudes of political leaders which determine whether they can interact in a way conducive to friendly relations between states. It is also the policies they adopt within their own states. The reason an apartheid state like South Africa became an international pariah stemmed from the problems it posed to international diplomacy, which only extremely insensitive white administrations in other states could ignore. It is, therefore, a requirement of international society that there is at least a semblance of non-discrimination against ethnic minorities that may form the dominant group in other states. This constrains statesmen to represent *all* their people, and not just the particular identity group from which they come.

Even provisions like the one I have just mentioned, and related ones such as the conventions which confer the right to a refugee status on anyone in fear of persecution for various reasons including race, are to be explained, I am suggesting, in terms of the conditions required for international society and, in particular, those needed to make the role of statesman effective. Such demands stem, not from ideals which may not be widely shared, but from what is found necessary for the performance of a role in which people with different personal values have to deal with each other. This, I suggest, can be generalised to the requirements of all ethical roles: their moral force is independent of any further values which adherence to them realises.

What has led to the opposite view is the influence of Enlightenment thinking at the end of the eighteenth century, which heralded, especially in the thought of Kant, a revival of cosmopolitanism. This is essentially a progressive doctrine aimed at questioning accepted roles and the particularistic obligations they imply. Simply to accept them is, Kant asserts, a sign of 'self-incurred immaturity',[24] from which we can escape if only we grasp the freedom to think for ourselves. Kant grants that in 'a particular *civil* post or office' one must simply conform to its rules, but that should not stop us questioning, as a thinking person holding the office, whether these rules are well founded. Even a clergyman, he suggests, is free 'in his own person' to criticise the doctrines which, as 'a servant of the church',[25] he is obliged to teach. All that is needed for such questioning, Kant maintains, is the use of reason. The problem is, of course, as critics of Kant, at least since Hegel, have pointed out, that reason alone seems to offer no substantive alternative to the moral demands our roles make of us. One role may make different demands on us from another and prevent us from fully identifying with it, but that is a very different matter from questioning them from outside all roles.

It is, perhaps, no accident that Kant equates the criticisms the clergyman makes 'in his own person' with those he makes 'as a scholar'.[26] But scholarship is a role with its own requirements, not, as Kant and, one fears, many other philosophers, have supposed, a socially uncontaminated expression of the workings of reason. To suppose that it is fosters the illusion that a critique of the ethics of a role can be made from a philosophical standpoint outside of it, rather than from a position within which is sensitive to its special demands. The danger of cosmopolitanism, then, is that it corrupts the politics of role by importing standards of performance that do not derive from the role-holders' own sincere attempts to apply the standards that the roles themselves prescribe. In this respect cosmopolitanism is no better than an identity politics that releases people from the requirements of transcultural roles. Both subordinate them to supposedly superior ends with, I have argued, consequences inimical to peace.

Notes

1. See my *Terrorism, Security and Nationality* (London: Routledge, 1994), pp. 161–72.
2. E.g. A.J. Coates, *The Ethics of War* (Manchester: Manchester University Press, 1997), pp. 278, 283.

3. Cp. James Tully, *Strange Multiplicity: Constitutionalism in an Age of Diversity* (Cambridge: Cambridge University Press, 1995), ch. 4.
4. Cp. Charles Blattberg, *From Pluralist to Patriotic Politics* (Oxford: Oxford University Press, 2000), chs 3–4.
5. Blattberg would not wish to term this 'accommodation' since conflict is hereby 'overcome', ibid., p. 120.
6. Though for a powerful argument that inequality is the cause of international terrorism see Ted Honderich, *After the Terror* (Edinburgh: Edinburgh University Press, 2002).
7. See Charles R. Beitz, 'Sovereignty and Morality in International Affairs', in D. Held (ed.), *Political Theory Today* (Oxford: Polity, 1991), p. 252.
8. Barry Buzan, *People, States and Fear* (New York: Harvester Wheatsheaf, 1991), p. 176.
9. This is the overall conclusion of Donald C. Horowitz, *Ethnic Groups in Conflict* (Berkeley: University of California Press, 1985).
10. And, indeed, leading to actions contrary to a group's interests: cp. John McGarry & Brendan O'Leary, *Explaining Northern Ireland* (Oxford: Blackwell, 1995), pp. 296–8.
11. A good example is provided by the treatment of Roma and similar peoples.
12. Cicero, *De republica* (many translations), I 25.
13. Cicero, *The Offices* (many translations), I 7.
14. Ibid., I 11.
15. Ibid., I 22.
16. See Quentin Skinner, *Machiavelli* (Oxford: Oxford University Press, 2000), ch. 2.
17. St Augustine, *The City of God* (many translations), IXX 7.
18. Ibid., II 21.
19. Ibid., IXX 23.
20. Ibid., II 21.
21. Ibid., IXX 24.
22. Hedley Bull, *The Anarchical Society* (Houndmills: Macmillan, 1977), chs 1–2.
23. Directorate of Human Rights, *Human Rights in International Law* (Strasbourg: Council of Europe, 1985), p. 55.
24. Immanuel Kant, 'An Answer to the Question: "What is Enlightenment?"', in H. Reiss (ed.), *Kant's Political Writings* (Cambridge: Cambridge University Press, 1970), p. 54.
25. Ibid., p. 57.
26. Ibid., p. 57.

Index